THE HOLY SPIRIT
IN CHRISTIAN THEOLOGY

THE
HOLY
SPIRIT IN
CHRISTIAN
THEOLOGY

by
George S. Hendry

Philadelphia
THE WESTMINSTER PRESS

Library of Congress Catalog Card Number: 56–7371

Foreword

In 1945 the Alumni Association and Board of Trustees of the Austin Presbyterian Theological Seminary established a lectureship, bringing a distinguished scholar each year to address an annual midwinter convocation of ministers and students on some phase of Christian thought.

The Thomas White Currie Bible Class of the Highland Park Presbyterian Church of Dallas, Texas, in 1950, undertook the maintenance of this lectureship in memory of the late Dr. Thomas White Currie, founder of the class and president of the seminary from 1921 to 1943.

The series of lectures on this foundation for the year 1955 is included in this volume.

DAVID L. STITT,
President.

Contents

Preface

The first three chapters of this book were put together when I was invited to give the C. C. Hein Memorial Lectures at the seminaries of the American Lutheran Church in Columbus, Ohio, and Dubuque, Iowa. Before I had time to revise the manuscript, I received an invitation to deliver the Thomas White Currie Lectures at the Austin Presbyterian Theological Seminary in Austin, Texas; and as this call came at relatively short notice, it seemed to present a suitable opportunity to develop some further aspects of the same theme. The Executive Committee of the American Lutheran Church readily consented to my incorporating the material I had given them in the larger series.

The book does not pretend to offer a systematic doctrine of the Holy Spirit. Its purpose is merely to direct attention to certain doctrinal problems in this area which have emerged in recent theological thought. I have come more and more to the view that the real core of many controversial issues is the implied doctrine of the Holy Spirit, and I have tried in these pages to consider some of them from this angle.

I wish to express my thanks for the many kindnesses shown to me at the three institutions at which the lectures were delivered.

G. S. H.

I

The Holy Spirit
and Christ

It has become almost a convention that those who undertake to write about the Holy Spirit should begin by deploring the neglect of this doctrine in the thought and life of the Church today. It may at once be said that this neglect (if it is a fact) is not due to willful indifference; for no one can read the testimony of the New Testament to the presence and power of the Spirit without wishing that it might be known in fuller measure in the experience of the Church in our time. Nor is it due to inattention to the doctrine of the Holy Spirit on the part of theologians; for many studies, historical and doctrinal, have been devoted to the subject, as the shelves of our theological libraries bear witness. The real reason is that the doctrine of the Holy Spirit is beset with difficulties and obscurities, which baffle the mind, and which no book has yet been able to dispel. The hope has been expressed that someday, someone, out of a fuller experience of the Spirit than is known among us, will write a great book about the Spirit, a book that " rings the bell." [1] I should hesitate to pronounce this a vain hope; but if such a book were to be written, it will not be one which answers all the questions and solves all the problems. Here it is true, as with no other topic in theology, that we see through a glass darkly. The true doctrine of the Holy Spirit will always be one that recognizes the inherent subtlety and complexity of the subject

11

and is most conscious of its inadequacy to grasp the mystery after which it gropes.

There are three particular reasons why we should not cherish too sanguine expectations:

1. When we say " spirit," we mean life, whatever else we may mean. Vitality is of the essence of spirit. Life is the ultimate mystery, which defies reduction to a formula; we may point toward it and describe it, but in the end it must speak for itself. Life begins beyond the point at which our words leave off. If the Holy Spirit means the living action of God in the world (and we can accept this as a provisional definition), our formulations cannot hope to catch up with the reality.

David Friedrich Strauss described the doctrine of the Holy Spirit (in one specific aspect) as the Achilles heel of Protestantism. In a sense the description is true. This is indeed the vulnerable point, the chink in the armor of our systems, which no argument from first principles can seal over. But it may be equally well, if less elegantly, described as the snorkel, the breathing tube which we reach out to the vivifying breath of God so as to avoid suffocation in the systematic shells of our own construction.

2. We have to recognize that the testimony of Holy Scripture, on which we principally depend, does not form a consistent and homogeneous pattern. We must disabuse our minds of the prejudice, common among those who hold Scripture in high esteem, that all its utterances on any one subject must be consistent with one another and that any real discrepancy would be incongruous with its divine authority. This is a prejudice, because it is without warrant in Scripture itself, which, as the record of a living experience, bears the authentic stamp of a rich diversity.

Moreover, the Bible itself is witness that there is no area

[margin handwritten notes:] Spirit = life and life cannot be reduced to words. Life the ultimate mystery.

The Holy Scripture does not present a unified doctrine of the Spirit

in which it is more necessary to practice discrimination than that of experience of the Spirit. According to Paul, one of the gifts of the Spirit is, paradoxically, " the ability to distinguish between spirits " (I Cor. 12:10 R.S.V.). It is impossible to frame a doctrine of the Holy Spirit by taking all the data indiscriminately and forcing them into the Procrustean bed of a formal system. We have to discriminate between what is true and what is false; we have to discriminate between what is primary and what is secondary, between what is central and what is peripheral; we have to discriminate between testimonies concerning the Spirit which reflect different levels of apprehension, between those which belong to different stages of the divine economy, and between those which have relation to different moments in the dialectic of spirit. I shall return to this in a moment, when I come to the question of method. But first I must refer to the third source of our difficulty.

We must distinguish between the various levels at which references to the Holy Spirit are found.

3. The dogmatic tradition of the Church (on which we are dependent, whether we acknowledge it or not) offers little clarification in this matter. In contrast to the elaborate care and precision which were applied to the definition of the doctrine of the person of Christ, the definition of the doctrine of the Holy Spirit, which was made at the Council of Constantinople in 381 and which has scarcely been improved upon since, is singularly meager, and might even be described as slipshod. I shall say more about this at a later stage, but I may remark at this point that a definition of the Church's faith regarding the Holy Spirit that omits explicit reference to the relation between the Spirit and the incarnate Christ, and to the relation between the Spirit and the Church, must be held to be gravely defective by the standard of the New Testament. And if the two great divisions in Christendom, that between East

Traditional theological statements are inadequate on the subject of the Holy Spirit.

and West, and that between Roman Catholicism and Protestantism, may be traced back to profound differences in regard to those two questions, the ultimate responsibility belongs to the undivided Church, which spoke so vaguely and so hesitatingly in the fourth century. At all events, the unhappy consequence is that any attempt at greater precision in regard to those questions brings us into controversy with those from whom we are divided.

In view of these difficulties it is scarcely necessary for me to add that it is not my intention in these chapters to offer an exhaustive treatment of the doctrine of the Holy Spirit. It is of a more modest and preliminary character: it is to try to determine what must be the basic pattern of a Christian doctrine of the Holy Spirit; and I want to do this by concentrating on some of the specific problems that have to be considered within its framework.

Author's purpose.

There are five problems that specially call for attention. (1) There is the problem that arises directly out of the New Testament witness to the Spirit — the problem of the relation between the Spirit and Christ. (2) There is the problem that presented itself to the mind of the Church in the fourth century as the sequel to the Christological decisions — the problem of the relation of the Spirit and God, or the Trinitarian problem. (3) There is the problem that has exercised theology more particularly in the West, since it lies at the root of the great divisions of Western Christendom — the problem of the relation between the Holy Spirit and the Church. (4) There is the problem that arises out of the Protestant answer to (3), which has figured prominently in our own Reformed tradition — the problem of the relation of the Spirit and the Word. (5) Finally, there is the problem that is suggested by certain strains in the Old Testament witness to the Spirit — which

Problems which the author has undertaken to discuss.
(5)

has engaged special interest in modern times, though it has been present to the mind of the Church at other times — the problem of the relation between the Holy Spirit and the human spirit.

It need hardly be said that these problems cannot be sealed off in separate compartments or considered in isolation from one another. It is obvious that one leads into the other and that, in the last analysis, they must be different aspects of one and the same problem. In distinguishing them, as we cannot avoid doing, we shall endeavor to light up the central problem from the perspective of each of them in turn.

We are, however, confronted with a problem of discrimination right at the outset: In what order should we take up these problems? This is more than an academic question of method; the answer we give will go far to determine the ultimate pattern that emerges. The choice is between two orders, which may be described as the canonical and the chronological, respectively. By the canonical order I mean that which follows the order of canonical Scripture, which takes first those aspects of the nature and activity of the Spirit which appear in the Old Testament, and regards them as the foundation or framework within which the material offered by the New Testament is to be understood. Strong arguments can be produced in favor of this order. In prefixing the Old Testament to the New in the canon of Christian Scripture, the Church appeared to suggest that in the study of our faith we should begin with Genesis and work our way through to Revelation. Moreover, if men's understanding of the Spirit has undergone a progressive development, this would appear to be the scientific way to elucidate it. This is the order that has been followed in the majority of

What order shall we use?

Canonical.

Though popular, Hendry doesn't favor it.

recent works on the Holy Spirit: the authors have approached their task by seeking to reach a general conception of the nature and activity of the Spirit, largely with
the aid of certain strains in the Old Testament which point
to a general presence and operation of the Spirit in creation and the life of man, and then they have endeavored
to find within this framework a place for the special emphasis of the New Testament on the gift of the Spirit. I do
not believe that this is satisfactory. The witness of the New
Testament to the gift of the Spirit is soteriological and
eschatological in character; when the attempt is made to fit
it into the framework of a conception that is cosmological
and anthropological in character, it almost certainly loses
something of its distinctiveness.[2]

The alternative order is the chronological, by which I
mean the order in which the problems engaged the attention of the Church. The Church did not begin with a general conception of the Spirit in the context of the relation
between God and the world or God and man; it began
with an endeavor to understand the distinctively Christian experience of the Spirit as a gift in the context of the
mission and work of Christ, and it was from this foundation that the doctrine of the Spirit was built up. But, if
we adopt this foundation, how can we find a place on it
for those more general aspects of the activity of the Spirit
to which the Old Testament bears witness? We seem to
be in a dilemma.

I do not believe, however, that the difficulty is insoluble.
It will be a main part of my thesis in these chapters that
if we approach the problems in the chronological order
(which is also the order in which I have enumerated
them), it will not only assist our understanding of the
structure of the Christian doctrine of the Holy Spirit, but

it will also provide a perspective from which we may see light on the wider aspects of the problem.

The New Testament testimonies to the Spirit may be divided, roughly, into two groups: (1) those of the Synoptics and The Acts, which are concerned principally with the incidence of the Spirit; and (2) those of the Epistles and the Fourth Gospel, which are more concerned with the functions and the nature of the Spirit. There is not, of course, a clear-cut division between the two groups; both interests converge, notably in the Fourth Gospel, where we have the most fully developed teaching on the work of the Spirit and at the same time the most explicit emphasis on the place of the Spirit in the economy of salvation.

[margin note: N.T. testimonies to the Spirit.]

The incidence of the Spirit is interpreted in the New Testament as the fulfillment of Old Testament prophecy, which had given a place of central importance to the Spirit in the eschatological hope of Israel. In the latter days of Israel's history, when the visitation of the Spirit had ceased to be known as a present reality in the life of the people and had become an object of future hope, this hope received a definite shape in the prophecy of an outpouring of the Spirit which would be permanent and universal. In contrast to the heroes, kings, and prophets of the past, upon whom the Spirit came only as an occasional and temporary visitant, the promised shoot of the stem of Jesse is one upon whom the Spirit of the Lord will *remain* (Isa. 11:2). Permanent endowment with the Spirit is also a prominent feature in the portrait of the Servant of the Lord in Second Isaiah:

[margin note: The Spirit interpreted by N.T as the fulfillment of the O.T. eschatological hope.]

"Behold my servant whom I uphold; mine elect, in whom my soul delighteth; I have put my Spirit upon him; he shall bring forth judgment to the Gentiles. . . . He shall not fail nor be discouraged; till he have set judgment in the earth: and the isles shall wait for his law " (Isa. 42:1–4).

The expectation of the inspired Messianic king or Servant of the Lord leads on to the vision of an outpouring of the Spirit upon the whole people of God and ultimately upon all flesh. The wish expressed by Moses that God would put his Spirit upon all the Lord's people (Num. 11:29) becomes a recurring feature of the prophetic eschatology. According to Ezekiel (ch. 36:26–28) and his dramatic vision of the valley of dry bones (ch. 37:1–14), the hope of the Spirit is the essential ground of the renewal of Israel. And the high point is reached in the prophecy of Joel:

" And it shall come to pass afterward, that I will pour out my Spirit upon all flesh; and your sons and your daughters shall prophesy, your old men shall dream dreams, your young men shall see visions: and also upon the servants and upon the handmaids in those days will I pour out my Spirit " (Joel 2:28 f.).

According to the New Testament, the fulfillment of both these aspects of the prophetic hope is found in Jesus and his Church.

1. The dual character of the prophetic hope sheds light on a feature of the New Testament that has given rise to some perplexity: while the Spirit figures prominently in the life and thought of the Primitive Church, it scarcely appears as a theme in the Synoptic teaching of Jesus. If the explicit and extensive teaching on the Spirit, which is ascribed to Jesus in the Fourth Gospel, has any historical basis, it is certainly difficult to understand why no trace of it should appear in the Synoptics. When we examine the Synoptics on their own account, however, it becomes clear

Spirit important to primitive Church, but hardly heard among the words of Jesus in Synoptics.

that their primary concern is to present Jesus, not merely
as a teacher of the Spirit, but as the unique bearer of the *Synoptics*
Spirit, the one in whom the prophetic hope of a permanent *do, however,*
presence of the Spirit is fulfilled. Although virtually ab- *present*
sent from the Synoptic teaching of Jesus, the Spirit is *Jesus as*
mentioned at decisive points in his life and ministry — at *one totally*
his conception, his baptism, his temptation, his first preach- *possessed*
and direct-
ing, his casting out of demons, and perhaps also at his *ed by the*
death on the cross. Taken together, these references make *Holy Spirit.*
it plain that the intention of the Synoptics is to present the
life of Jesus as one wholly possessed and directed by the
Spirit.

It is impossible for me to go through all these references; but it will suffice if I confine my attention to the
reference to the visible descent of the Spirit at the bap- *At his*
tism of Jesus, which is reported in similar terms by all *baptism,*
three Synoptics, and which is clearly meant to be regarded *Jesus*
as an event of fundamental importance. A careful reading *was shown*
of the three narratives will show that the emphasis is not *to be*
so much on the *descent* of the Spirit as on the visible *the per-*
revelation of it: the Spirit is *seen* descending upon him like *manent*
a dove ("in bodily form," Luke 3:22). In other words, *bearer*
the point is not that the Spirit descended upon Jesus at *of the*
that precise moment (having not been upon him before), *Spirit.*
but that it was then revealed that Jesus is the permanent
bearer of the Spirit. (The question to whom the revelation
was made is not of primary importance.) There is no support in the passage for an adoptionist Christology, which
rests upon a misconception of its central motif. Although
the phrase, "Thou art my . . . Son," was used as a formula of adoption, its conflation with the phrase applied to
the elect servant in Isa. 42:1 indicates that its source is to
be found in the Second Psalm, and that the intention of

the voice from heaven is to *identify* Jesus as the one to whom these testimonies of Scripture apply, not to suggest that he was at that moment being elected to the Messianic office. Further, the association of the descent of the Spirit with the baptism of Jesus has a revelatory rather than an adoptionist significance: by the visible descent of the Spirit upon him at his baptism Jesus is identified as the one who will dispense the Spirit and inaugurate the distinctively Christian baptism. This is, of course, the interpretation of the whole episode given in the Fourth Gospel (although the baptism of Jesus is not explicitly recorded there): the visible descent of the Spirit is divinely revealed to John as the sign that Jesus is the permanent bearer and dispenser of the Holy Spirit:

> " And John bore witness, ' I saw the Spirit descend as a dove from heaven, and it remained on him. I myself did not know him; but he who sent me to baptize with water said to me, " He on whom you see the Spirit descend and remain, this is he who baptizes with the Holy Spirit." And I have seen and borne witness that this is the Son of God ' " (John 1:32–34).

2. The second element in the prophetic hope, the fulfillment of which is proclaimed in the New Testament, is the general outpouring of the Spirit " upon all flesh." It is the prophecy of Joel which forms the text of Peter's discourse on the Day of Pentecost (Acts 2:16 ff.).

There is a well-known difficulty here. The Fourth Gospel gives an account of the outpouring of the Spirit that conflicts with that of the Pentecost narrative. According to the Johannine account (John 20:22), the gift of the Spirit was imparted directly from the mouth of the risen Lord to the assembled disciples (Thomas being absent) on the evening of Easter. Easter and Pentecost are, so to speak, telescoped together. In the Lucan account, on the other hand,

[handwritten margin note: The voice from Heaven was only to identify Jesus as the One of whom the Scripture spoke. No evidence of Adoption-ism]

they are separated by a well-defined interval. We need not
concern ourselves with the historical problem raised by this
discrepancy or with the attempts that have been made to
harmonize the two narratives. There is one point on which,
it should be noted, both of them are in agreement: the
gift of the Spirit comes at the end — or after the end — of
the earthly ministry of Jesus. The point is emphasized in
Luke by his twice recording the ascension (Luke 24:51
and Acts 1:9) and the Lord's command to his disciples to
wait (Luke 24:49 and Acts 1:4). There is no period of
waiting in the Johannine account of the insufflation. Yet
the Johannine teaching is even more emphatic that the
coming of the Spirit is consequent on the departure of
Christ. The point is stated categorically — almost harshly
— in the Evangelist's comment on a somewhat cryptic
utterance of Jesus at the Feast of Tabernacles: "Now this
he said about the Spirit, which those who believed in him
were to receive; for as yet the Spirit was not [given], because Jesus was not yet glorified" (John 7:39). It is re-
iterated with great emphasis in the Paraclete sayings: the
presence of Jesus, which was only temporary, must be
withdrawn, in order that the Spirit may come to stay forever. The alternation is expressed or implied in all five
sayings, and most explicitly in John 16:7, where Jesus almost seems to present his disciples with a choice between
his continued presence and the coming of the Paraclete:
"Nevertheless I tell you the truth: it is to your advantage
that I go away, for if I do not go away, the Paraclete will
not come to you; but if I go, I will send him to you" (John
16:7).

Here, then, is the first thing that must be set down in
answer to the question, What is the relation between the
Spirit and Christ? The Spirit is *after* Christ in the divine

[right margin handwritten note:] Both the synoptics and the Johannine Gospel agree that the gift of the Spirit come after the end of Jesus ministry

Jesus' presence must be withdrawn that men might receive the Spirit.

economy; the earthly ministry of Christ must be completed before the Spirit comes.

This New Testament emphasis on the economic order or sequence appears to lend support to the view which commended itself to some in the ancient Church, when the problem arose of defining the relations between God, Christ, and the Spirit. It was the view of the Modalists that it is the same personal subject with whom we have to do in each case; the difference lies only in the modes in which he has been present and active in the world, first as Father, secondly as Son, and thirdly as Holy Spirit. It is a plausible view, especially as regards Christ and the Spirit; and, indeed, it contains an element of truth, for the presence of the Spirit is truly the continued presence of Christ in another mode. It is impossible that Christ's promise, " Lo, I am with you always, even unto the end of the world," can refer to anything other than his presence in the Spirit; and there is no evidence that the Early Church ever thought otherwise. The manner in which Paul describes the Christian situation indifferently as " in Christ " and " in the Spirit " shows that he drew no distinction between the presence of the Spirit and the presence of Christ. And in the Johannine teaching, the Spirit, as " another Paraclete," is to be to the disciples what Christ himself was to them while he was present with them, and the presence of the Spirit is to be equivalent to the presence of Christ himself. According to one widely accepted view of John 14:18, and its relation to what precedes, the coming of the Spirit is to be the coming of Christ.

This, however, does not mean that the presence of the Spirit, or of Christ in the Spirit, supersedes the historical presence of Christ, in the sense that it renders the earthly ministry of the incarnate Christ of no further significance.

In so far as it holds or implies that the dispensation of the Spirit supersedes the historical manifestation of God in Christ, modalism strikes at the basis of the Christian faith, which rests on the decisiveness and finality of the incarnation. The work accomplished by Christ in his incarnate life remains central, and it cannot be superseded. Thus, although the presence of the Spirit is equivalent to the presence of Christ, it is necessary at the same time to observe the distinction between them. The presence of the Spirit is always secondary to, and consequent upon, the presence of the incarnate Christ. It is Christ, and not the Spirit, who became incarnate and wrought in history the work of God for the salvation of men. The function of the Spirit is essentially subservient and instrumental to the work of the incarnate Christ.

This distinction is a prominent feature in the teaching of the Fourth Gospel, notably the Paraclete sayings. The Spirit does not come into operation until Christ is glorified, i.e., until he has completed the work of his ministry and returned to the Father. This is because the work of the Spirit is essentially of a reproductive nature; it has always to do with the work of the incarnate Christ. The Paraclete sayings lay marked stress on the unoriginality of the Spirit's work: this work, if we may so express it, is simply to hold the spotlight on Christ, to glorify him by taking what is his and showing it to his disciples (John 16:14). The Spirit is to be remembrancer (ch. 14:26), not innovator. This is not contradicted by the passage in the fifth Paraclete saying, which promises that the Spirit will lead into all *the* truth (the article must not be disregarded); for the truth, in the idiom of the Fourth Evangelist, is the truth that came by Jesus Christ (ch. 1:17), the truth which was given to him in its fullness by the

[handwritten marginal note:] Modalism supposedly holds that the giving of the Spirit was more important than Jesus' ministry. (This doesn't seem essential to the modalist position) John — The work of the Spirit is primarily to provide a secondary continuation of the ministry of Christ.

Father (ch. 16:15), and of which he said, "I am . . . the truth" (ch. 14:6). It will be the office of the Spirit to declare this truth, not because he originates it, but because he hears it, and only as such is he the Spirit of truth (ch. 16:13). In a word, it is the function of the Spirit, according to the Johannine teaching, to re-present the truth that is in Christ.

In the Pauline writings the relation between the Spirit and Christ appears in much the same dialectical pattern of identity and distinction. Christ and the Spirit are so closely associated in the life of Christians that their names are interchangeable. The Christian standing, as we already noted, can be described equally well as " in Christ " (Rom. 8:1) and "in the Spirit" (Phil. 2:1). In Gal. 3:1, 2 Paul puts the receiving of the Spirit on a par with the decisive encounter with Jesus Christ which initiates the Christian life, and in Rom. 8:9 he states that the possession of the Spirit is the *conditio sine qua non* of being a Christian. From the point of view of Christian experience there was evidently no distinction for him between the presence of Christ and the presence of the Spirit. Yet it would be a mistake to conclude that Paul identified the Spirit with the exalted Christ, despite what appears to be a categorical affirmation of their identity in II Cor. 3.17, " Now the Lord is the Spirit "; for " the Lord " here refers to " the Lord " of the preceding sentence, which is clearly an echo of Ex. 34:34, and the " is " is exegetical (*est = significat,* as in Eph. 4:9).[3] The meaning is that, as turning to the Lord is shown by Scripture to have been the condition for the removing of the veil from the face of Moses, so it will be for those who read " Moses " today; only, the Lord to whom they must turn is not to be sought on Mount Sinai, but in his presence in the Spirit. The thought is of a " dy-

*Paul –
The
Spirit
very
similar
to, but
not the
same as,
Christ,
Himself.*

namic identity"; [4] the Lord " is " the Spirit in the sense
that he is present and active in the Spirit among men. It
should also be noted that in the second half of the same
sentence Paul refers to the Spirit *of* the Lord, and this is
the mode of language which he commonly employs to
designate the Spirit in relation to Christ, e.g., the Spirit of
Christ (Rom. 8:9; Gal. 4:6; Phil. 1:19), the Spirit of his
[God's] Son (Gal. 4:6). The use of the preposition " of "
clearly points to a close relationship between the Spirit and
Christ, and equally clearly it points to a distinction between them. What is the nature of this distinction? In the
Fourth Gospel, as noted, the chief emphasis is laid on the
temporal sequence: the Spirit is subsequent to Christ.
Paul nowhere stresses this point, perhaps because it had
become self-evident; his thought is rather of a distinction
between the respective spheres of operation of Christ and
the Spirit, which may be described as the objective and
the subjective respectively; the Spirit is the subjective
complement or counterpart of the objective fact of Christ,
and it is the function of the Spirit to bring about an inner
experience of the outward fact in the hearts of men.

This does not mean that the objective fact is dissolved
into a subjective experience; there remains a polarity between them (the importance of which we shall see in another context). The fact of Christ is primarily a fact of
history, and as such it is reported (Gal. 3:1) and attested
(I Cor. 1:1, 2) in the apostolic preaching. The hearing of
this report is the indispensable condition of faith (Rom.
10:17). Faith, however, comes only when the outward fact
penetrates to the inner heart of man and takes possession
of him there — and this is the work of the Spirit. " No one
can say ' Jesus is Lord ' except by the Holy Spirit " (I Cor.
12:3). This is the reason for Paul's insistence that the

Paul-
also
states
that the
role of
the Holy
Spirit is
to re-
create
the min-
istry of
Jesus
Christ for
the
believer.

Faith,
however,
comes
only after
the hist-
orical
facts pen-
etrate to
the heart
of a man.
This = work
of Spirit.

communication of Christ does not depend on human eloquence or wisdom, but on "the demonstration of the Spirit and of power" (ch. 2:1-4). The human means might, at best, effect a knowledge of Christ as a historical figure (perhaps this is what Paul meant when he spoke of knowing Christ "after the flesh" or "from a human point of view," II Cor. 5:16); only the Spirit can open the door to a real, inner apprehension of the Lordship of Christ.

Difference between John & Paul basically a difference in perspective

The difference between Johannine and the Pauline conceptions may be described as a difference of perspective. The author of the Fourth Gospel, assuming the standpoint of a contemporary of the incarnation, presents the relation of the Spirit to Christ chiefly in terms of continuation; Paul, from the standpoint of a later time, presents the experience of the Spirit, which is known to him and his contemporaries, as the complement to the fact of Christ. These two emphases, it is clear, are themselves complementary: the Spirit continues the presence of Christ beyond the brief span of his historical appearance and completes it by effecting its inward apprehension among men.

Definition of the work of the Spirit

In both emphases, however, the Spirit is presented in a purely Christocentric reference. There is no reference in the New Testament to any work of the Spirit apart from Christ. The Spirit is, in an exclusive sense, the Spirit of Christ.

This is the central feature in the New Testament witness to the Spirit. In itself it is perfectly clear and intelligible; but when we begin to reflect on it, it presents certain difficulties. The first is this: If the Holy Spirit is in an exclusive sense the Spirit of Christ, does this mean that the New Testament recognizes no presence or activity of the Spirit in the world prior to the historical advent of Christ? That would seem to follow from the insistence of the New

Testament on the novelty of the Spirit. Yet, while the
coming of the Spirit is undoubtedly hailed as a novel feature of the eschatological era that has dawned with the
coming of Christ, it is evident that the novelty is to be
understood to pertain, not to the coming of the Spirit as
such (unless it be in relation to the long interval which
had elapsed since the Spirit, as was commonly believed,
had departed from Israel with the extinction of the prophetic line), but rather to the novel features of the Pente-
costal outpouring, its permanence and universality. Still,
this does not meet the real difficulty: <u>If the work of the
Spirit is related exclusively to the historical work of the
incarnate Christ in the New Testament, how is it possible
to speak of an activity of the Spirit before the advent of
Christ?</u> Clearly, it is possible only if that activity is related
to the advent of Christ prophetically or proleptically. And
this, we find, is precisely the position. <u>All the New Testament references to the activity of the Spirit prior to the
incarnation have to do with words of Old Testament Scripture, which are interpreted as prophetic of the historical</u>
advent.

I have said " words of Old Testament Scripture " rather
than simply " the Old Testament," because when we have
regard to the actual use of the Old Testament by the
writers of the New, this mode of expression seems more
accurate. It is often said that the New Testament writers
assume the " inspiration " of the Old Testament as a
whole,[5] and while it is true that there are some passages
and phrases that point in this direction, it is gratuitous to
assume that this view is present in every instance. There
is no subject on which people are more prone to harbor
preconceived ideas than inspiration; it is of the highest importance, therefore, that we should look at the New Testa-

[margin handwritten note:] If the work of the spirit is basically a continuation of the ministry of Jesus Christ, how can the spirit have existed before the birth of Christ? Prophetically.

ment teaching carefully and without prejudice.

There is one strong argument for the popular view that the New Testament writers accept the inspiration of the Old Testament as a whole: It is that this was an accepted belief in contemporary Jewry, and the New Testament writers, being themselves Jews, may be presumed to have shared it. But those who put forward this argument overlook the fact that there was a strong reason why the New Testament writers should be critical of Jewish belief precisely in this particular: It is that orthodox Jewry, taking its stand on the Old Testament as the inspired word of God, had rejected Christ. The crux of the matter for the first Christian generation, confronted with unbelieving Judaism, was the interpretation of the Old Testament. In other words, they were concerned, not so much with how the Old Testament was written, as with how it was read, and it was in the reading of the Old Testament, which found in it testimony to Christ, that they saw especially the work of the Holy Spirit. This is made very plain in II Cor., ch. 3, where Paul comes closest to a formal treatment of the problem: The Old Testament becomes a dispensation of condemnation and death to those who read it in the synagogue, not because it is devoid of splendor, but because its splendor is concealed from them by the veil which is over their minds; it is the Spirit that removes the veil and discloses the splendor of the Old Testament, which is none other than the splendor of the Lord.

It is also important to note that in their actual use of the Old Testament the New Testament writers are highly selective; and while we have in two late passages what appear to be blanket affirmations of the inspiration of the Old Testament, most of the writers of the New Testament do not ascribe inspiration except to certain passages or

[margin handwritten note: First century Christians critical of Jewish Biblical interpretation because this had led them to reject Jesus.]

strains in the Old Testament which bear prophetic testi- *As a*
mony to Christ.[6] According to the Fourth Gospel, it is the *result*
searched Scriptures that testify of Christ (John 5:39), and *of this*
in the Lucan account of the walk to Emmaus, it is the *mistrust,*
things *in* all the Scriptures concerning himself which the *the early*
risen Christ interprets to the two disciples (Luke 24:25). *Christians*
The inspiration of these passages is not something apart *became*
from their testimonial significance, but in fact coincides *highly*
with it. The Spirit of prophecy is identified with the Spirit *selective*
of Christ and correlated with the Spirit of the apostolic *as to*
kerygma in I Peter 1:10–12. Thus the action of the Spirit *which*
is literally Christocentric, inasmuch as it is always cen- *passages*
tered on Christ, whether it come from before or after the *of the*
incarnation. There is a difference of distribution and de- *O.T. they*
gree, but none of focus. The New Testament knows no *considered*
work of the Spirit except in relation to the historical mani- *to be*
festation of Christ. *inspired.*

It remains only to mention one other aspect of this exclusiveness: The New Testament contains no trace of the *Thus,*
conception of the Spirit as the principle that animates the *before*
life of man as God's creature. Paul does recognize a human *or after*
spirit, but he does not posit any ontological relation be- *the birth*
tween it and the Spirit of God; the Spirit of God is always *of Christ,*
a gift that comes from God and testifies to the human *the Spirit*
spirit of the salvation that God has wrought in Christ. *could alway*
be shown
to witness
to Christ-
at least
in the
prophetic
(see p. 27)
sense.

II

The Holy Spirit
and God

In the New Testament the Spirit is in a pre-eminent sense the Spirit of Christ; the mission of the Spirit is consequent upon the incarnation, and all the functions of the Spirit are instrumental to the historical work of Christ. But as Christ is the revelation of God in history, the Spirit must also stand in some relation to God. It is significant that Paul calls the Spirit the Spirit of God and the Holy Spirit much more often than the Spirit of Christ. The question must now be asked, What are the mutual relations between the Spirit, Christ, and God?

It is now generally acknowledged that the doctrine of the Trinity is not found in the New Testament. At the same time, it is more commonly recognized than it has sometimes been, that the New Testament contains the materials out of which the doctrine of the Trinity took shape; and these are to be found, not so much in the texts in which the names of the three " persons " occur together (although the number of these is not insignificant), as rather in the outlines of a Trinitarian pattern which can be discerned, especially in the thought of Paul and the Fourth Evangelist.

I

In the Fourth Gospel, the introduction of the Spirit as " another Paraclete " (John 14:16) points to a parallel between the Spirit and the Son, which is developed with

reference to their respective missions: As the Son was sent
by the Father (v. 24 and often), came forth from the
Father (ch. 16:28), so the Spirit is given by the Father
(ch. 14:16), sent by the Father (v. 26), and proceeds from
the Father (ch. 15:26). Always, however, the mission of
the Spirit is in some way mediated through the Son: The *The Father*
Father sends the Spirit in response to the prayer of the *is present*
Son (ch. 14:16), and in his name (v. 26), or the Son sends *and active*
the Spirit from the Father (chs. 15:26, 16:7). The Spirit *in the Son,*
continues and extends the mission of the Son (chs. 14:26, *and the*
15:26, 16:13 f.), and as such works in that field which is *Son is*
common to the Father and the Son (ch. 16:15). There is *present*
thus a functional or dynamic identity between the Spirit *in the*
and the Son, and, ultimately, the Father: The Father is *Spirit.*
present and active in the Son, who in turn continues to be
present and active in the Spirit.

It is in this sense that we must understand the saying of
Jesus to the woman of Samaria, " God is spirit " (ch. 4:24).
Since this saying was uttered in reply to the woman's question about the right place to worship, it has commonly
been taken to mean that God, being Spirit, is present
everywhere and can be worshiped anywhere; the important thing is not where men worship, but how they worship. This interpretation involves the assumption that the
implied contrast to spirit is matter, or body (which is local-
ized). But the Johannine contrast to spirit, like the Pauline, is flesh (cf. ch. 3:6); and flesh connotes everything
that belongs to the human realm, everything that is possible or accessible to man. " God is spirit," then, so far
from meaning that God is present and accessible everywhere, means the precise opposite; it means that God is
present in his own realm, to which man as such has no
access. To worship God in spirit is not a possibility that is

always and everywhere open to man, in virtue of a supposed affinity of spirit between man and God which is independent of locality; for this precisely there is not — man is flesh and God is Spirit. But this is just the gospel of Christ, that this possibility has now been opened to men; God has made himself accessible to them; the Word has become flesh; the truth has come by Jesus Christ: "But the hour is coming, and now is, when the true worshipers will worship the Father in spirit and truth, for such the Father seeks to worship him" (ch. 4:23). The point, then, is not that locality has ceased to have any relevance to worship; still less is it implied that locality never had any relevance to it, for Jesus declares categorically, "Salvation is from the Jews" (v. 22). The meaning is that the location has been redefined, and God is now to be worshiped in the place where he is present, i.e., in Him who is the truth incarnate, and who dramatically announces to the woman, "I who speak to you am he" (v. 26). God actively seeks men to worship him in spirit and truth by making himself accessible to them in his Son, who is the truth incarnate, and by the mission of the Spirit, who is the Spirit of the truth. The worship of God in spirit and truth, is therefore, Trinitarian worship: it is to worship God through Jesus Christ, in the Holy Spirit.[1]

The same Trinitarian pattern appears, somewhat more distinctly, in the thought of Paul. God is the ultimate source of the Spirit, as he is the sender of the Son, with whom the Spirit is so closely associated: "God has sent the Spirit of his Son into our hearts" (Gal. 4:6). Paul, however, has a more definite conception of the nature and function of the Spirit in the context of his theology of revelation. He interprets the Spirit of God, on the analogy of the human spirit, as God's knowledge of himself:

John 4.

Only through Christ can man find God, and only through the Spirit can man find Christ.

"For the Spirit searches everything, even the depths of God. For what person knows a man's thoughts except the spirit of the man which is in him? So also no one comprehends the thoughts of God except the Spirit of God" (I Cor. 2:10 f.).

Paul does not develop this conception further; for his interest is not in the fact that God knows himself, but in the fact that he shares that knowledge with others, by giving them his Spirit. The dominant thought is always of the Spirit as going out from God to others — as in the passage immediately following: "Now we have received not the spirit of the world, but the Spirit which is from God, that we might know . . ." (I Cor. 2:12).

The dominate thought in Paul is of the Spirit of God as going out from God to others.

The Spirit, which is *from* God, or "proceeds" from God, makes God known to us, because the Spirit is God's knowledge of Himself, and we can know God only as he shares his self-knowledge with us. But God does not make himself known to us by the immediate impartation of his Spirit; the gift of the Spirit is inseparably bound up with the mediation of Christ. It is when we consider the respective roles of Christ and the Spirit in the self-revelation of God that the Trinitarian structure of the Pauline theology comes most clearly in sight. The gospel, as Paul proclaims it, is centered in Christ; his theme is Christ crucified (I Cor., chs. 1; 2). The message of Christ crucified is gospel, because this is an event in which God was at work: "God was in Christ reconciling the world unto himself" (II Cor. 5:19). Christ is the personal revelation of God; the love of God is personally expressed in him (Rom. 5:8; 8:39); the glory of God is present in his face (II Cor. 4:6). Paul consistently distinguishes between God and Christ, and he never ascribes to God the historical actions and experiences of which Christ was the subject. But since those actions and experiences derive their evangelical significance from the fact that God was the ultimate author of them, Christ may be described as the self-expression or self-objectification of God in history.

The realization of God's saving purpose with men, however, requires that they should recognize and respond to his expression of himself in Christ, and that, as Paul saw, is humanly impossible. For in becoming incarnate Christ divested himself of the form of God and was found in human form (Phil. 2:5–8). The incarnation meant the assumption of an incognito, as Kierkegaard expressed it; Christ appeared as a man among men, a figure of history, and, of course, he could be known as such, whether by personal acquaintance or by report. But so to know him was to know him "after the flesh"; it was to know him only as "the princes of this world" knew him; for if they had truly known him, "they would not have crucified the Lord of glory" (I Cor. 2:8). To know Christ truly, i.e., to know God in Christ, it is necessary to see him, so to speak, from God's point of view; and this is precisely the office of the Spirit, as Paul understands it. The Spirit constitutes the subjective condition which is necessary for the apprehension and recognition of the objective self-manifestation of God in Christ; for the Spirit is God knowing himself, and to receive the Spirit is to participate in that knowledge.

The work of God in the gospel has for Paul a dual aspect: there is the (objective) fact of Christ, in whom God confronted men, and there is the (subjective) gift of the Spirit, by which men recognize and respond to the gift of God in Christ. Both are essential. "The knowledge of the glory of God" which shines "in the face of Christ" becomes luminous to us only when God kindles a corresponding light within our hearts (II Cor. 4:6). The love of God

[Margin handwritten notes:]

Paul:
To see Christ from God's point of view is our gift from the Holy Spirit

Paul:
Only by the Spirit can men recognize and respond to the objective (see p. 25, note II) fact of God's gift in Christ.

is objectively demonstrated and extended to us in Christ: " God shows his love for us in that while we were yet sinners Christ died for us " (Rom. 5:8). But the subjective experience of — or reaction to — this proffered love is the work of the Spirit: " The love of God has been poured into our hearts through the Holy Spirit which has been given to us " (Rom. 5:5). Our adoption as sons of God, effected objectively in the mission and work of Christ, is consummated when God sends "the Spirit of his Son into our hearts, crying, Abba! Father! " (Gal. 4:4–6).

The much discussed order of clauses in the apostolic benediction becomes intelligible when it is viewed in this light. The prime fact of the gospel is the objective mission of Christ and his giving of himself for us: " The grace of the Lord Jesus Christ." This fact, however, has a transcendent content and significance; for God was in Christ: " The love of God." And the gift of the love of God, which is expressed in the grace of the Lord Jesus Christ, is received and realized by participation in the gift of the Spirit: " The communion of the Holy Spirit." The same order appears in another passage:

"But we are bound to give thanks to God always for you, brethren beloved by the *Lord*, because *God* chose you from the beginning to be saved, through consecration by the *Spirit* and belief in the truth " (II Thess. 2:13).

The love of the Lord (i.e., Jesus Christ) is the objective reality with which we are confronted; it has its transcendent ground in the divine election, and it elicits recognition and response in us by the Spirit.

The paradoxical combination of unity and diversity in which God, Christ, and the Spirit appear in the theology of Paul clearly indicates its Trinitarian character. The unity is primarily of a functional nature: "The Spirit is and gives nothing other than what Christ is and gives and what God is and gives." [2] The distinction between them relates to their respective spheres of activity. God is the ultimate source and author of the whole movement: "All this is from God" (II Cor. 5:18). God's love and salvation is given objective expression in the world in Jesus Christ, "whom God put forward . . . to show his righteousness" (Rom. 3:25). The subjective recognition and acceptance and response to the divine advance is the work of the Holy Spirit in our hearts. But the essential unity of the whole movement is such that the names of the three "persons" are interchangeable; for since God was in Christ, every relation to Christ is at the same time a relation to God; and since the Holy Spirit is the Spirit of God and of Christ, the presence of the Spirit in us is equivalent to the presence of God (Eph. 2:21) and of Christ (Rom. 8:9 f.). And the gifts of the Spirit are at the same time the ministrations of Christ and the operations of God:

"Now there are diversities of gifts, but the same Spirit. And there are diversities of administrations, but the same Lord. And there are diversities of operations, but it is the same God which worketh all in all" (I Cor. 12:4–6).

II

It is a common reproach that when the Christian Church came to formulate its faith in the era of the great councils, it introduced subtleties and complexities that go beyond anything to be found in the New Testament. The main occasion of this reproach is, of course, the Chalcedonian definition concerning the person of Christ. The Church's defense in this matter has always been that it was only by these careful elaborations that it was able to guard the

[handwritten margin note: The names of God, Christ, & Spirit are interchangeable, so that the presence of the Spirit also assures the presence to God & Christ.]

essential elements of the New Testament faith against
perversion by heretics. This reproach, if it is a reproach,
can certainly not be leveled at what the Church had to say
about the Holy Spirit. Rather the contrary. <u>If the Church
went considerably beyond the New Testament in defining
the doctrine of the Person of Christ, it fell considerably
short of the New Testament in defining the doctrine of the
Holy Spirit</u>. This deficiency deserves special attention, for
it was to have fateful consequences.

The Church's faith in the Holy Spirit was defined at the
Second General Council at Constantinople in 381.[3] The
Creed of Nicaea, where the First General Council was
held in 325, had been content with a bare mention of the
Holy Spirit. But when Arian sympathizers, in retreat from
the Nicene decision on the consubstantiality of the Son
with the Father, transferred their attack to the Spirit, it became necessary for the Church to define its position on
this question more explicitly. The bald statement of the
Church's faith, promulgated at Nicaea, was expanded to
read:

" And [we believe] in the Holy Spirit, the Lord and Life-
    giver,
  who proceeds from the Father,
  who with the Father and the Son is together worshiped
    and together glorified,
  who spoke by the prophets." [4]

As a formulation of the Christian faith concerning the
Holy Spirit, this statement is patently defective, both by
the standard of the New Testament and in comparison
with the second article of the Creed in which it is in-
corporated. In view of the close affinity between the Arians
and the Pneumatomachians, who have been called the
Arians of the Spirit, it might have been expected that the

article of the Creed which was directed against the latter would follow closely the pattern of that directed against the former. But there is no more striking feature of the Niceno-Constantinopolitan Creed than the profound difference in style and tone between the second and third articles. Three things are noticeable — and puzzling — about the third article:

1. The divinity of the Holy Spirit is strongly — but only indirectly — suggested; it is not explicitly affirmed. Various explanations have been offered for this — the widespread dislike of the term *homoousios,* which was used at Nicaea, the conciliatory purpose of the emperor in summoning the Council, perhaps even some uncertainty on the matter in the minds of several of the orthodox Fathers.[5] Still, the reticence of the Creed here remains puzzling, when compared with the bold and emphatic declarations of the second article ("true God from true God . . .").

2. The most glaring — and fateful — defect of the Creed is the absence of any statement concerning the relation of the Holy Spirit to Christ. And this is accentuated by the third thing:

3. The sole reference to the work of the Spirit concerns the inspiration of the Old Testament prophets. Doubtless this was intended as an indirect affirmation of the preexistence of the Spirit; but it tends to throw into relief the absence of any reference to the distinctively New Testament work of the Spirit.

For these reasons it was scarcely to be hoped that the Creed of Constantinople, although "it is the only one for which ecumenicity, or universal acceptance, can be plausibly claimed . . . one of the few threads by which the tattered fragments of the divided robe of Christendom are held together,"[6] would fully satisfy the mind of the

[margin handwritten note:] Most glaring ommission of the Creed was any, omention of the relation of the Spirit and Christ was ommited.

Church concerning its faith in the Holy Spirit. Its deficiencies sowed seeds of discontent, which were to ripen in tragic controversy.

The most serious deficiency, as has been noted, concerns the relation of the Spirit to Christ. There is, indeed, a parallelism between Christ and the Spirit, which is seen in their common derivation from the Father and their association together with the Father as objects of Christian worship and devotion. But of the Christocentric character of the mission and work of the Spirit, which is so strongly emphasized in the New Testament, there is not a hint. The basic relationship of the Spirit is defined as "procession from the Father." This, of course, has a firm Scriptural warrant; it is taken literally (with only a change of the preposition) from John 15:26. But why should this point have been singled out for mention? Why was no mention made of the part played by Christ in the gift of the Spirit, a part to which reference is frequently made in the Paraclete sayings, and indeed in the selfsame verse that speaks of the procession from the Father:

No mention of the Christo-centric mission of the Spirit.

"But when the Paraclete comes, whom I shall send to you from the Father, even the Spirit of truth, who proceeds from the Father, he will bear witness to me" (v. 26).

The omission is strange in a *Christian* creed; and what makes it stranger is that there is no evidence of any intention to exclude the participation of Christ. On the contrary, the writings of the Fathers both before and after Constantinople abound in passages where reference is made to both the Father and the Son in connection with the procession of the Spirit. Sometimes the phrase is, "From the Father and the Son"; sometimes, "From the Father through the Son"; the latter, adopted by John of

Damascus, became the standard formula in the Eastern Church. The Western Church, however, was not content with a tacit understanding of the participation of the Son in the gift of the Spirit; it took the bold step of altering the Creed by inserting the phrase, " And from the Son " (*filioque*) after the words, "Who proceeds from the Father." [7]

This Western interpolation was one of the chief factors that precipitated the final breach between the Eastern and Western Churches which took place in 1054 and remains unhealed to this day. It was the subject of protracted and acrimonious debates which went on for many centuries both before and after the breach, and which failed to lead to agreement.[8]

It is hard to understand how so fine a point of Trinitarian theology as the doctrine of the " double procession " should have aroused such feeling as it did at the time of the schism, and it is probable that the ostensible meaning of the *filioque* concealed another which related it more intimately to the actualities of Christian faith and experience. It is significant that the interpolation was (in all probability) first made in the liturgical use of the Creed; it was not the product of theological deliberation — indeed, the responsible theological organ of the Church resisted the interpolation for centuries. Here *lex orandi* was *lex credendi*. The *filioque* was a fruit of Christian devotion, and if its persistence and eventual triumph bear witness to the strength of the root from which it sprang, it is hardly conceivable that that root was enthusiasm for the doctrine of the double procession, an abstruse theologoumenon which is not likely to have been intelligible even to the average ecclesiastic. It seems much more probable that it was a general sense of the inadequacy of the Creed to ex-

press the distinctively Christian apprehension of the Holy
Spirit as the Spirit of Christ.

In the experience of the Church the presence of the
Holy Spirit was known, not as an alternative to, but as a
mode of, the presence of the living Christ which forms the
constitutive fact of Christian faith — a fact that is enshrined in the primitive Christian confession, " Jesus Christ
is Lord." The presence of the Spirit does not supersede the
presence of Christ: that is the spiritualist heresy which
has plagued the Church repeatedly from the time of Mon-
tanus onward. The faith of the Christian Church is always
centered in Christ, in whom God was reconciling the world
unto himself, and its evangelical assurance rests in the
finality of his work, accomplished once for all in history,
and effectually re-presented through the Spirit. In other
words, the Christian experience of the Holy Spirit has as
its specific content the encounter with the living Christ in
the power of his finished work. The Christian Church has
from the first been exposed to the danger of an undefined,
unregulated, and, in the final count, unevangelical spirituality. Warnings against it are given in the New Testament, which defines the test of authentic Christian spirituality as confession of the incarnate and risen Christ
(I John 4:1–3; I Cor. 12:3).

While the association of the Spirit with Christ prevents
the dissolution of Christian faith into a general religiosity,
it also conserves its essentially personal character. Despite
the spirituality of Christian faith, there is no place in it for
mysticism — at least not for mysticism of the classical type,
in which the frontiers of personal distinctness are blurred.
Christian experience consists in encounter with a personal
Lord, and as such it has an indelibly personal character.
(It involves a personal responsibility and therefore an

[Handwritten marginal notes:] In the experience of the Church, the Holy Spirit was known, as a mode of the presence of the Living Christ. If mysticism be viewed as an encounter with God which blurrs human personality there is no room for Xianity which insists on personal encounter between Man & God.

ethic. Mysticism has no ethics, but only a technique for acquiring the mystical experience.) That is why the personality of the Spirit is important for faith; as Kähler has pointed out,[9] this is not because faith is concerned to affirm that the Spirit is a person in relation to God, but because it is concerned to affirm that the Spirit is a person in relation to us, i.e., that the Spirit is not merely a divine influence or force, but that in the Spirit God meets us and deals with us personally. Without the personal work of the Spirit we could have Christ only as an impersonal memory. It is the living person of God, present in his Spirit, that unites us with Christ and through him deals personally with us.

III

If this is the real meaning of the *filioque*, how is it related to its ostensible meaning? Does the distinctively Christian apprehension of the Holy Spirit as the Spirit of Christ necessarily involve the doctrine of the double procession? The case for the *filioque* has been presented powerfully in contemporary theology by Karl Barth, and an examination of his main arguments may serve to point up some of the difficulties involved.[10]

Barth defends the *filioque* with the following arguments:

1. He holds it to be the fundamental rule of Trinitarian theology, which is for him the ground of revelation, that "pronouncements on the reality of the divine modes of existence ' antecedently in themselves ' cannot be different in content from those that have to be made about their reality in revelation." [11] As it is more summarily expressed by Welch, " we must make the doctrine of immanent Trinity conform exactly in content to the economic Trinity." [12] So, if the Spirit who operates externally upon us is the

Spirit of the Father and the Son, he can be no other than
the Spirit of the Father *and the Son* in the internal relations of the immanent Trinity. If the procession of the
Spirit is from the Father alone (as Photius insisted the
Creed should be interpreted — the so-called "monopa-
trist" position), we have then a discordance between the
relation of the Spirit to the Son in the economy of revelation and that which subsists in the inner life of the Trinity,
between God as he is in himself and God as he is revealed
to us.

2. Barth interprets the Holy Spirit, on the Augustinian
pattern, as the love that constitutes the essence of the communion between the Father and the Son, and he contends
that this communion in the inner, divine life of the Trinity
forms the ground of the communion between God and
man, which is established in revelation through the Holy
Spirit. Did this communion in the inner life of the Trinity
not exist antecedently — and there would be no room for
it if the Spirit proceeds from the Father alone — the communion of the Spirit between God and man would lack
objective content and ground.

3. Barth fears, conversely, lest the denial of the *filioque*
in respect of the immanent Trinity might open the door to
a corresponding interpretation of revelation, according to
which the Holy Spirit would be understood in a one-sided
manner as the Spirit of the Father, having a mission in the
world separate and distinct from the mission of the Son.
Barth is emphatic that the God to whose fellowship we
are admitted by the Holy Spirit is none other than the God
and Father of our Lord Jesus Christ, the God who has revealed himself in his saving work; in other words, our only
access to God is on the basis of the reconciliation wrought
in Christ. The consequence of denying the *filioque*, Barth

The God into whose fellowship we are admitted by the Spirit, is none other than the / God & Father of our Lord, J.C.

fears, would be that Christ is bypassed and the relation between God and man is viewed primarily in the Creator-creature aspect and assumes a naturalistic and unethical character. Welch puts it this way:

" We must say certainly that God's being Holy Spirit depends upon his being Son as well as Father. For the Christian experience of the Holy Spirit, while now independent of Christ's physical presence, is not independent of his having lived in the flesh. And the test of the presence of the Holy Spirit, as distinguished from other spirits, lies in the fact that this Spirit is the Spirit of Christ, gives the mind of Christ, works through love, and testifies to Christ. Otherwise the conception of the Holy Spirit degenerates into only a vague notion of divine immanentism or spiritism." [13]

Let us look at these arguments more closely. The first depends for its force on Barth's contention that the doctrine of the Trinity is rooted in the fact of revelation. I cannot go into this here.[14] But granted it is true, granted the validity of the rule Barth derives from it, viz., that there must be a correspondence between the internal relations of the persons of the Trinity and those which are manifested in their external operations, must this correspondence be exact in every detail? Barth's contention really delivers a powerful weapon into hands of those who argue that defenders of the double procession of the Spirit ought in consistency to maintain the double generation of the Son; for since the Creed explicitly mentions the office of the Holy Spirit in connection with the external mission of the Son ("was incarnate from the Holy Spirit"), there would seem to be even stronger ground for the interpolation of a *Spirituque* in the clause which speaks of his eternal generation, " begotten of his Father before all worlds." Yet Barth follows the tradition of Western theology in strenuously resisting this inference.

The second argument, viz., that the communion be-

sages in the New Testament assign to him a central role in this work (e.g., John 1:3 f., Heb. 1:2 f., Col. 1:15 f.). It was a vital element in the faith of the New Testament that the historical revelation and work of Christ was instrumental to the realization of the whole purpose of God in creation, and the writers express this by affirming that the mediator of salvation was also the mediator of creation: in him, or through him, God created the world. But a difficult question arises here: In assigning to the Son the role of mediator of creation, precisely whom did the New Testament writers have in mind? Was it the eternal Son, the discarnate Word (*logos asarkos*), the second person of the Trinity as such; or was it the Son who was destined in the counsel of God to become the Word incarnate and who stood before the eternal eye of God as Jesus the Christ, clothed in our humanity and bearing our sin? In other words, does the Son fulfill two distinct and unrelated roles as mediator of creation and mediator of salvation; or is he already from all eternity cast in the role of mediator of salvation and as such the mediator of creation? Barth maintains the latter view, and in so doing he goes so far as to characterize the whole conception of the discarnate Word or " second person of the Trinity " as an abstraction, which, while indispensable to Trinitarian theology, barely appears in the New Testament. The New Testament, says Barth, never thinks of the pre-existent Christ in detachment from the concrete content of his mediatorial work.[21] His conclusion is, therefore, that the Son through whom God made the world is none other than the Saviour, and that " the purpose and meaning of creation is to make possible the history of God's covenant with man, which has its beginning, middle, and end in Jesus Christ." [22]

We are on more difficult ground when it comes to defining the role of the Holy Spirit in the Trinitarian work

[handwritten marginal note: Christ instrumental through- out whole of worlds history, & ergo, also His Spirit was active at creat- ion.]

of creation. The New Testament contains no direct reference to it at all; the only exegetical basis for it there is to be found in those few passages which characterize the Spirit as the author or source of life (John 6:63; I Cor. 15:45; II Cor. 3:6). The primary reference in all these passages, as Barth is constrained to acknowledge, is to the *new* life that has been brought to men, who were dead in sin, through the work of Christ and faith in him; but he detects in them an echo of those Old Testament passages (especially Gen. 2:7) where the Spirit of God appears as the source of man's very existence and, indeed, of that of all living creatures, and he proceeds to argue that while the New Testament writers, in interpreting the life-giving work of the Spirit in a soteriological-eschatological sense, look beyond the cosmological or biological sense which it bears in the Old Testament, they at the same time subsume the latter under the former; they regard the Spirit, through whom the purpose of God with his creatures is realized, as the *conditio sine qua non* of their creaturely existence; in other words, they recognize no life in the creature apart from that which has been brought to light by the gospel of the resurrection.[23]

In this way Barth seeks to maintain the principle of the *filioque;* but the interpretation presents serious difficulties. The most obvious is this: If the Spirit of God animates the creaturely existence of man, there must be a sense in which it can be said that all men who exist have the Spirit; but the New Testament is emphatic that the Spirit is a novel gift to the Church, consequent upon and complementary to the work of the incarnate Christ. This feature of the New Testament witness is inevitably blurred if the Spirit that animates is identified with the Spirit of the Father and the Son.

[left margin annotations:]

No supporting biblical data for pre-existant Christ.

If spirit animates man, it must be an inherant part of man's make-up. This is contrary to N.T. witness.

Barth attempts to meet this difficulty in his doctrine of
man by defining more precisely the sense in which man
has Spirit. According to Barth, man, who is God's creature,
owing his existence to God and destined for fellowship
with God, is not without God. No matter what his own
attitude to God may be, even though he be an atheist, it
remains true that he is not without God. This relation of
man to God, however, is not something inherent in the
constitution of man; it consists in God's free activity toward man. Man is in virtue of the fact that God is for him.
Now this activity, this movement of God toward man, according to Barth, is what is meant by Spirit; and thus the
fact that man *is* can also be expressed in this form: Man
has Spirit. It must not be said that man *is* Spirit, because
Spirit is never his own possession but always comes to him
as a gift. Man is, inasmuch as God gives him his Spirit. As
the principle of his relation to God, Spirit is the ground
of his being as man. But, says Barth, this function of the
Spirit is itself grounded in the basic meaning of the Spirit
as that element or factor by which man is brought into
covenant fellowship with God. And thus, as the new man
in the covenant lives by the fact that God gives him his
Spirit, so also does the natural man: " It is the same Spirit
that is for the one the principle of his renewal and for the
other the principle of his creaturely reality." [24]

In this interpretation, it seems to me, Barth is obliged
to evacuate the concept of Spirit of one of the principal
elements which belong to it in the New Testament, viz.,
the element of subjectivization. The Spirit, as Barth himself emphasizes in an earlier part of his work, constitutes
the subjective factor in the event of revelation; it is by the
Spirit that men apprehend and receive and respond to the
revelation of God; it is by the Spirit that the objective

[Handwritten marginalia:] According to Barth, no man is without God.

[Handwritten marginalia:] The Spirit is the means by which men apprehend and respond to God. Barth identifies the Spirit with man's subjectivity

event of revelation becomes subjective.[25] But there is no question of a subjective element in the work of the Spirit as "the principle of man's creaturely reality." On the contrary, Barth expressly eliminates it. Spirit here signifies a movement which proceeds strictly and exclusively from God to man; it has nothing whatsoever to do with man's subjectivity.[26] It is difficult to understand how Barth can maintain the identity of this inarticulate Spirit with the Spirit of the New Testament, whereby we cry, "Abba! Father!"

It should scarcely be necessary for me to add that in describing the Spirit as the principle of man's creaturely existence Barth has assigned to the Spirit a role which the New Testament and traditional Trinitarian theology assign to the Son or Word. It is he, "the second person in the Trinity," who represents the movement from God, in which man's creaturely existence is grounded. The Spirit, on the other hand, represents the movement toward God which reciprocates the former. In Barth's anthropology the Spirit reduplicates the role of the Son, and the distinction between them, which underlies his defense of the *filioque,* disappears. The external operations of the Trinity are not only undivided — they have become indistinguishable.

The difficulties which arise, both from acceptance and from rejection of the *filioque,* would seem to indicate, as I have suggested elsewhere,[27] that it was a false solution to a real problem. It satisfied the immediate concern of the Christian mind to identify the Spirit that is known in the experience of salvation as the Spirit of Christ, but it raises grave difficulties when it is extended to the operations of the Trinity in creation. The problem will meet us again in another form in the final chapter of this book.

[Margin note, handwritten:] Hendry: Spirit comes from God and cannot, as Barth claims, be an inherent part of man's nature.

III

The Holy Spirit
and the Church

I begin with three quotations:

"Different beliefs about the Church are rooted in different beliefs or unbeliefs about the Holy Spirit."[1]

"Many of our disagreements about the nature of the Church will be further clarified by renewed investigation of the New Testament relationship between the Holy Spirit and Christ, the Holy Spirit and the Word, as well as the Holy Spirit and the Church.[2]

"In our work we have been led to the conclusion that it is of decisive importance for the advance of ecumenical work that the doctrine of the Church be treated in close relation both to the doctrine of Christ and to the doctrine of the Holy Spirit."[3]

When we take up the question of the relation between the Holy Spirit and the Church, it is clear that we are entering one of the most controversial areas of current theological discussion in the ecumenical field. And when we think of the magnitude and complexity of the issues involved, it is also clear that we cannot hope to achieve much by way of clarification in a brief chapter. Yet I believe it is possible to establish one fundamental point from which we may survey the problem and appraise the various positions taken.

In both quotations from Faith and Order reports, it is suggested that the problem of the Holy Spirit and the Church must be considered in relation to the doctrine of

Christ. This is incontestably true, but I think it needs to be formulated in a more precise way if we are to get it in proper focus. What do we mean by the doctrine of Christ? The doctrine of Christ, in the primary New Testament sense, means the gospel — that series of events which God wrought in Christ for the salvation of the world. There has come into being within recent years a new appreciation — I might almost say a rediscovery of the significance of the concept " gospel," chiefly through the labors of New Testament scholars; we have been taught to see that the theme of the apostolic preaching was not a system of ideas or a portrait of an ideal figure; it was a sequence of acts in which God's eternal purpose for men was definitively accomplished in history. It was, I think, the present bishop of Durham who first pointed out that this must be our starting point in the study of the Church.[4] Dr. A. M. Ramsey sought to show that the Church arose from the gospel, and that its nature and structure can be understood only in the light of the gospel of Christ crucified and risen. His further argument that the order of the " catholic " Church, and, in particular, the episcopal ministry, enshrines or expresses essential elements of the gospel I believe to be untenable, but I am sure he is right in his main contention that the whole question of the Church must be studied in the light of the gospel.

We shall have this in mind when we come to the specific question with which we are concerned, the relation between the Holy Spirit and the Church. Broadly speaking, we can distinguish three views which are taken of this relationship, the Roman Catholic view (with which we may associate the very similar Anglo-Catholic view), the view of the Protestant Reformation, and the Spiritualist or Enthusiast view.

The whole question of the Church must be studied in the light of the Gospel.

I

The Roman Catholic view is succinctly expressed in the official formula: The Holy Spirit is the soul of the Church. This formula, promulgated by Leo XIII,[5] has more recently been endorsed by Pius XII.[6] Some theologians are careful to explain that the term "soul" is here employed analogically; it is not to be taken to mean that the Holy Spirit is the soul of the Church in the same sense as our souls are the souls of our bodies. He is not actually "the interior form of unity in the Church." The immanent principle of the Church, it is explained, is found in the gifts of the Spirit, especially faith and charity, but as it is the Spirit who bestows these gifts and makes them operative in the Church, He may fittingly be described as the animating and unifying principle of the Church.[7]

R.R.C. The Spirit is that which enables the church to carry out its continuation of the ministry of Christ on earth.

This conception fits into the basic view of the relation of the Church to Christ that is held in Roman Catholicism. In the Roman view, the Church is primarily the successor of Christ; the presence and power of the Holy Spirit are then regarded as endowments bequeathed by Christ to the Church to enable it to discharge its supernatural role. The Roman conception is presented very clearly in the following passage from the Encyclical *Satis cognitum,* of Leo XIII:

"The Son of God assumed human nature . . . and thus living on earth he taught his doctrine and gave his laws, conversing with men.

And since it was necessary that his divine mission should be perpetuated to the end of time, he took to himself disciples, trained by himself, and made them partakers of his own authority. And when he had invoked upon them from heaven the Spirit of truth, he bade them go through the whole world and faithfully preach to all nations what he had taught and what he had commanded, so that by the profession of his doctrine and the observance of his laws, the human race might attain to holiness on earth and never-ending happiness in heaven." [8]

Two things are noteworthy about this conception. (1) The disciples are viewed exclusively in the role of successors to Christ; his mission, which is left incomplete by him at his departure,[9] devolves upon them. In the words of the present pope, " It is through them, by commission of the divine Redeemer himself, that Christ's apostolate as Teacher, King, and Priest is to endure." [10] And to this end they are endowed with his authority. The main emphasis, in Roman ecclesiology, is always on the *authority* which the apostles received from Christ and transmitted to the hierarchy of the Roman Church. This authority to teach (*munus doctrinale*), to govern (*munus regale*), and to sacrifice (*munus sacerdotale*), is described by the present pope as " the fundamental law of the whole Church." [11]

There is, no doubt, a certain measure of truth in the Roman Catholic view, and the Roman Catholic theologians can marshal an imposing array of texts from the New Testament to support it. There is a sense in which the mission of Christ is continued in the mission of the apostles: " As the Father has sent me, even so send I you " (John 20:21). There is a sense in which the gift of the Holy Spirit may be described as the divine principle of power and authority on which the apostolic mission of the Church depends. But in the Roman Church this dependence is understood as possession; i.e., the power and authority, which derive from the Holy Spirit, are held to be given to the Church itself to exercise; the Holy Spirit is regarded as the source or principle of the Church's power. It is clear that this is far removed from the way in which the situation was understood in the Church of the New

Testament. In the New Testament the authority of the Holy Spirit is an authority to which the Church remains subject; it is the principle of the Church's obedience. The Council of Constantinople showed a true instinct for the essential when it defined the first of the attributes of the Spirit as "Lordship"; for the Church of the New Testament did not experience the Spirit as an immanent principle by which it succeeded to the authority of its Lord but as a presence in whom its living Lord continued to exercise his own authority. The presence of the Holy Spirit was marked by the confession of the Lordship of Jesus (I Cor. 12:3), not the magisterium of the Church.

(2) The other feature of the Roman Catholic theory which should be noted is this. In the assumption that the mission of Christ is transmissible to his disciples, there is an implicit denial of the completeness and finality of the work of Christ, and, with that, a loss of its evangelical character; for what makes the gospel truly gospel is the fact that "it is finished"; God's decisive deed for the salvation of the world is done once for all and nothing needs to be added to it. In the Roman theory the evangelical note is inevitably lost, and the work of Christ assumes a legal character. It is significant that when the Roman theologians are seeking to prove the foundation of the Church by Christ, it is always to his teaching and his "legislation" that they point. Thus, for example, Pope Leo XIII, when he adduces the incarnation as the supreme instance of God's dealing with men, which is shown in the visibility of the Church, describes the content of the incarnation in these terms: " The Son of God assumed human nature . . . and thus living on earth he taught his doctrine and gave his laws." And to the question, What was Christ's purpose in founding the Church? he answers formally: "This: to

The idea that the Gospel of the Church completes the ministry of Jesus Christ suggests that Christ's work of revelation was incomplete.

transmit to it the same mission and the same mandate which he had received from the Father, that they should be perpetuated." [12] The real ground of the Church is the necessity of continuing the teaching and ruling office of Christ. The Church is not essentially related to the gospel; for in Roman Christianity there is no gospel. The basic constituents of the Church are the power of teaching and the power of jurisdiction; in the exercise of these powers the Church carries on "the same mission and the same mandate which he had received from the Father." Its empowerment to fulfill this mission derives from the Holy Spirit, who proceeds from this doctrinaire and authoritarian Christ, and who, as such, is a Spirit of authority.

It appears, thus, that in the Roman Catholic view the Holy Spirit fulfills a purely instrumental role in establishing a direct continuity between Christ and the Church. There is no place in the Roman Catholic system for a confrontation of the Church with the Holy Spirit as Lord, i.e., as witness to the Lordship of Christ over the Church. Rather, the Holy Spirit, as the soul of the Church, is the source from which the Church is inflated with its own authoritarian claim. Hence there is a loss of the sense of the "personality" of the Holy Spirit, which is rooted in the experience of confrontation with one who is Lord. In Roman Catholic theology the chief interest is always in the effects of the Holy Spirit, the gifts and graces that spring from his indwelling; the Holy Spirit is thought of as an impersonal principle, a source or channel of supernatural endowments, rather than a Lord and a Person. "This communication of the Spirit of Christ is the channel through which all the gifts, powers, and extraordinary graces found superabundantly in the Head as in their source flow into all the members of the Church, and are perfected daily in

[handwritten margin note: R.C.C. views the Spirit as a grab-bag from which it may derive its privileges and authority. For them, it is not a confrontation with the Spirit of God.]

them according to the place they hold in the mystical body of Christ." [13]

A further consequence of the Roman Catholic view of the relation of the Church and the Holy Spirit is the introduction of a radical distinction in the Church between those who exercise authority and those upon whom it is exercised. Roman Catholic theology is emphatic that "the Church must be a hierarchical society; the apostles and their successors must be the chiefs and rulers." [14] "That those who exercise power in this body are its first and chief members must be maintained uncompromisingly. It is through them, by commission of the divine Redeemer himself, that Christ's apostolate as Teacher, King, and Priest is to endure." [15] The pope is at pains to resist the inference that these bearers of the apostolic succession have a monopoly of the Holy Spirit. He stresses that the Holy Spirit "is personally present and divinely active in all the members," but he adds this qualification that "in the inferior members he acts also through the ministry of the higher members." [16]

R.C.C. Holy Spirit largely in the possession of the clergy.

Higher and lower members

This conception that the gift of the Holy Spirit to the Church is "channeled" through some of its "higher members" plays a prominent part also in Anglo-Catholic theory, and it is worth our while to look at it in the form in which it is presented by some of the members of that group. By far the most interesting presentation of the thesis is that of the bishop of Durham, to which I have already referred, and in which he attempts to find a basis for the episcopal structure of the Church in the nature of the gospel as such. The bishop appears to recognize that historical arguments cannot bear the weight that some of his friends attempt to rest upon them, and he appeals to them only in a secondary way to support a position that rests primarily on dogmatic grounds. "To burrow in the New Testament for forms of ministry and imitate them is archaeological religion: to seek that form of ministry which the whole New Testament creates is the more evangelical way. And our view of the ministry had better be evangelical than archaeological." [17]

According to this view, the meaning and structure of the Church are determined by the gospel of Christ crucified and risen. The Church is the body of Christ which is created by his dying and rising again, and in which his dying and rising again find continuing expression. To this end, it is argued, there must be in the structure of the body organs that have the special function of representing the gospel of Christ to the Church. This office, which originally belonged to the apostles, is now held by the bishops, who "are regarded as the successors of the apostles in office and as the organs of the Church's unity." [18]

In *The Apostolic Ministry*, a large volume of essays on the subject by a group of Anglo-Catholic scholars, published in 1946, the thesis was propounded that the apostolate represents the "essential ministry," and that this essential ministry is continued in the episcopate, which is thus "the repository of the commission which Christ gave to his apostles"; [19] it was further emphasized that the essential ministry, which is the guarantee of the Church's existence, is continued by the chain of episcopal succession apart from the continuity of the Church as a whole.

The plain implication of this view is that the Holy Spirit is not given to the Church, but is canalized alongside the Church. Anglo-Catholics are fain to deny this; e.g., Bishop Ramsey writes: "The succession of bishops is not an isolated channel of grace, since from the first Christ bestows grace through every sacramental act of his body. But cer-

[margin notes, handwritten:]
Anglicans

Bishops succeed the apostles as the organs of the Church's unity.

Bishops seem to have a corner on the Holy Spirit.

tain actions in this work of grace are confined to the
bishops." [20] When they contend, however, as even Bishop
Ramsey does, that episcopacy is of the *esse* of the Church,
it is impossible to resist the inference that the gift of the
Holy Spirit as such does not constitute the Church.[21]

In the New Testament the main emphasis is laid on the
common participation in the Spirit by all the members of
the Church. It is by this common participation in the Spirit
that they are baptized into one body. Within this unity,
however, and on the basis of it, there is room for considerable diversity of function, for the manifestation of the
Spirit, which is given to each individual within the unity
of the body, appears in a wide variety of charismatic endowments (I Cor. 12:4 ff.). It is the unity of the Spirit
which forms the *esse* of the Church; the charismatic diversity belongs to its *bene esse*. But Anglo-Catholicism
reverses this order; it takes one office, which belongs to the
order of charismatic diversity, and makes it of the *esse* of
the Church; it thus destroys the unity of the Church by
making a radical cleavage between the episcopal clergy
and the laity.

Two further questions emerge from this position. When
the episcopate (with or without the pope) is thus placed
on the side of Christ over against the Church and assigned
the exclusive function of re-presenting the gospel to the
Church, who re-presents the gospel to the bishop? If the
pope is the vicar of Christ to the world, who re-presents
Christ to the pope? The singular lack of provision for these
needs in both Roman Catholicism and Anglo-Catholicism
must be regarded as highly significant.

A similar question arises where emphasis is laid on the
bishop (or pope) as the custodian of the truth of the
gospel. It is the question that is always raised by such

[margin notes:]
Anglican
The gift of the Spirit does not constitute the Church.

N.T. places emphasis upon the common participation by all the members in the Spirit.

Who represents Christ to the bishop?

claims to custodianship: *Quis custodiet custodes?* "Who
will take care of the caretakers?" The claim can have no
more ultimate basis than the word of those who assert it
— the logical conclusion is the Roman dogma of papal in-
fallibility — for if it can be tested by reference to some objective standard, the claim becomes meaningless. This is
acknowledged with a candor bordering on naïveté by
Congar in his remarks on the use of the Vincentian canon,
quod ubique, quod semper, quod ab omnibus creditum est,
(" what has been believed everywhere, always, and by
everybody ") as a criterion of catholicity: " If this ' canon '
were really the standard of Catholicism, then the supreme
magisterium would rest with historians, for it is their busi-
ness to say, from *a study of the texts,* what has been believed always, everywhere, by everyone. The magisterium,
always living in the Church by the twofold principle of
the apostolic succession and the assistance of the Holy
Spirit, simply declares what *is* the belief of the universal
Church. The past may be known by the fact of the present;
the present is not determined by a reference to the past.
Here we touch upon a decisive issue between the Protestant Reformation and the Church, for the very idea of reformation is involved. Is the nature of the apostolic Church
such that, having fundamentally erred, she can be brought
back to the truth and reformed by professors in the name
of critical study? Protestantism only exists in virtue of an
affirmative answer to this question, justified by the Vincentian ' canon.' " [22] Congar proceeds to draw the astound-
ing conclusion that, while the apostolic magisterium
apparently confers upon its infallible bearer a license to
rewrite history, the Protestant attitude, which places some
reliance on the critical study of the historical records by
" professors," is based on the principle of private judgment!

*Roman
and Anglo
Catholicism
eliminate
private
Judgement*

II

The evangelical-Protestant understanding of the relation between the Holy Spirit and the Church, to which we now turn, is determined primarily by its concern for the integrity of the gospel. It is this concern that underlies its critical attitude to the " Roman Catholic " position in this matter. The fundamental objection to the Roman Catholic position is that it destroys the gospel by obliterating any distinction between the gospel and the teaching of the Church. In Roman Catholicism, as we have seen, the Church is to all intents and purposes the successor of Christ; it has inherited from him, through the apostles, " the same mission and the same mandate which he had received from the Father," and it has been endowed with the power of the Holy Spirit to enable it to fulfill it. The consequence is that the gospel is identified exclusively with what is spoken *by* the Church, and there is no provision whereby the gospel may be spoken *to* the Church. As Bishop Newbigin says, " the idea of 'the Word' practically disappears. There is still teaching (*didache*) as to what the Church believes and does. But there is no preaching (*kerygma*) of that Word by which the Church, not only initially but always, lives." [23]

The heart of the Protestant position is found in its conception of what may be called the abiding polarity between Christ and the Church. In the Roman Catholic view, this polarity belonged only to the initial relation between Christ and the twelve disciples, and on his departure it was immediately changed to a relation of continuity. In other words, the Twelve ceased then to stand to Christ in the relation of disciples to their Master; they themselves succeeded to his mastery, and to enable them

Roman Catholic Church obliterates distinction between the Gospel and the teaching of the Church.

R.C.C. The apostles become Christ.

Prot. the apostles follow Christ.

to exercise it they received the gift of the Spirit which is conceived as a miraculous, immanent endowment. Now, no doubt, the transition from discipleship to apostleship marked a decisive turn in the experience of the Twelve, but that it involved a turn of ninety degrees in their relation to Christ, as the Roman Catholic theory that they took over his mission requires, cannot be sustained by the evidence of the New Testament. According to the New Testament, the mission of Christ does not require to be taken over, for it is complete; what he accomplished is sufficient once for all. It requires only to be communicated to men; and this is the primary responsibility laid upon the apostles. They were appointed, not successors to Christ, but witnesses to him; their task was to point to him by recalling (*anamnesis,* I Cor. 11:24), proclaiming (*kerygma,* I Cor. 2:4), transmitting (*paradosis,* I Cor. 15:3), and testifying to (*martyrion* I Cor. 1:6) the salient facts of his mission. It is misleading, therefore, to speak of the mission of the apostles as a continuation of the mission of Christ, as if they were on the same level. The mission of the apostles remains subordinate and instrumental to the mission of Christ (in relation to which it might be more accurately described as a *com*mission). In other words, the apostolic function of the Twelve remains a *ministerium;* it does not become a *magisterium:* "We preach not ourselves, but Christ Jesus the Lord; and ourselves your servants for Jesus' sake" (II Cor. 4:5).[24]

The Roman Catholic theory that the apostolate takes over the mission of Christ is based on the ground that since his bodily presence was withdrawn, the apostles (as representing the Church) now constitute the body through which he acts vicariously. But the Roman Catholic interpretation obliterates any real distinction between the body and Him who acts through it; the polarity which existed between Christ and the Twelve is virtually fused into an identity. This is a conception which the teaching of the Johannine Christ on the coming of the Spirit seems almost to have been expressly framed to exclude. Take any authoritative statement of the Roman theory, such as that given by Leo XIII in the encyclical *Satis cognitum*,[25] and reduce its pontifical magniloquence to the simple style of the New Testament: it makes Christ appear to have said to his disciples, "When I go away, you will take my place." This, of course, is very different from what he did say. He promised that his place would be taken by the Spirit, (*allos parakletos*), toward whom the Twelve would stand in the same relation of polarity as they had stood to Christ during his bodily presence with them. The Spirit is the true vicar of Christ, Christ's *alter ego*, and was known as such in the Church by the fact that he was encountered in the same role of Lord (*Kyrios*) as Christ himself had been. In the Roman Catholic view the Lordship of Christ devolves upon the apostles, and the Holy Spirit is promised them as assistance in filling their lordly role. But according to the New Testament, the Holy Spirit is essentially Lord, because he only comes from him who is exalted as Lord by his triumph over sin and death (Acts 2:33). The role of the apostles is correlated with the work of the Spirit. It is their commission to bear witness to the Lordship of Christ. But it is not in their power to establish it among men, because it consists, not just in an authority to teach and to give commands, but in a work of salvation which he completed by his exaltation. They can confess it and testify to it; but without the testimony of the Spirit who comes from the exalted Lord, it cannot be established among men.

The Spirit is the true vicar of Christ.

It is the recognition of the Lordship of the Spirit and the abiding polarity in the relation between the Spirit and the Church that distinguishes the Protestant doctrine. From the Roman Catholic side the charge is sometimes brought against the Protestant doctrine that it fails to recognize the *immanence* or *indwelling* of the Spirit, which is a main feature of the New Testament, just as it fails to recognize the incarnation as " the real and actual gift of the divine life to human nature." Congar writes: "As a form of religion and of relation to Christ, and in him to the blessed Trinity, Protestantism has stopped short with John the Baptist and still awaits the fulfillment of the baptism of water and of the Spirit, and the gifts of the Spirit, first fruits of our heritage. It forgets that since John the Baptist, God is incarnate." [26] The Protestant rejoinder to this must be that Catholicism fails to recognize the Spirit who indwells as the Spirit who is *Kyrios,* the Spirit whose mission it is to bear witness to Christ. The Spirit who indwells the Roman Catholic Church bears witness to — the Church; it is a spirit that says, *Tu es Petrus,* not, *Kyrios Iesous* ("Jesus is Lord") (I Cor. 12:3). In the Protestant understanding the Spirit does truly indwell the Church; only he makes his indwelling presence known, not by inflating the Church with a sense of its own privilege and power, but by directing its attention to its living and exalted Lord and by exposing it to his grace. This is the reason why the locus of the Holy Spirit in the Church is defined more specifically as the " means of grace " (the Word, sacraments, and prayer) — i.e., precisely those functions of the Church in which it looks away from itself to Christ.[27] It is not that Protestantism does not take seriously the promise of Christ's continued presence with his Church by the indwelling spirit. Only, it understands the presence of Christ

The Spirit witnesses to Christ, but R.C.C. view of Spirit witnesses only to the Church

as a real *presence*, not a fusion of identity. When the Pauline figure of the body of Christ is pressed to yield the conclusion that "the Church is, as it were, another Christ,"[28] as is frequently done in Catholicism, it may be said with confidence that such a thought would have horrified the apostle, for whom the efficacy of the gospel depended upon the absolute pre-eminence of Christ (Rom. 1:4; Col. 1:18; 2:10). What we have by the *koinonia* of the Holy Spirit is the *grace* of the Lord Jesus Christ, his presence as an evangelical, saving presence — which it cannot be if there is any fusion or confusion of identity between Christ and the Church. Conversely, if the union between Christ and the Church were of an organic nature, the mission of the Holy Spirit would be redundant. The mission of the Holy Spirit does indeed effect the union between Christ and the Church, but in such a way that at the same time it attests the indelible distinction between them; it underscores the fact that the Christ who presents himself to the Church in the Holy Spirit is the Christ who died and rose again — "Christ clothed with his gospel," as Calvin expressed it.[29] It is this identity between the remembered Christ and the Christ present in the Spirit which is expressed in the Protestant doctrine of the means of grace. Thus, while Roman Catholicism interprets the Spirit as the soul of the Church and so blurs the distinction between Christ and the Church, Protestantism recognizes the Spirit as the Spirit of Christ, i.e., the Spirit in which Christ, remaining identical with himself, is present with his Church as Saviour and Lord.

III

It will serve further to clarify the Protestant doctrine if we proceed to consider the third main view of the rela-

tion between the Holy Spirit and the Church which has
been current in Christendom. This view is known by various names, spiritualism, enthusiasm, *Schwärmerei*; it is the
view represented in its extreme form by the Anabaptists
of the Reformation period and held in modified forms by
those Churches which trace their ancestry from the Anabaptists. Since the Anabaptist movement arose on the soil
of the Reformation (though its roots may go further back),
its enthusiasm is sometimes taken to be a trait of Protestantism as such; but while Anabaptism and Protestantism
were alike opposed to Rome, there was a radical difference
between them in their understanding of the Holy Spirit,
and, as everyone knows, Luther's opposition to the Anabaptists was scarcely less bitter than his opposition to
Rome.

Enthusiasm exalts the sovereign freedom of the Spirit
over against the Roman Catholic tendency to canalize and
domesticate the Spirit in the Church, but in such a way as
virtually to sever the connection between the mission of
the Spirit and the historical Christ. The emphasis is laid
on the immediate, subjective experience of the Spirit in
the individual rather than on his appropriation of " the
redemption purchased by Christ " in the work of his incarnate life. The real attitude of enthusiasm (and this was
openly avowed in its more extravagant forms such as Mon-
tanism and Joachimism) is that the dispensation of the
Spirit superseded the historical revelation of Christ. This
is concealed in modern forms of enthusiasm beneath an
appearance of devotion to the Christ of the New Testament, but it is not really changed; for the historical revelation of Christ is treated as the stimulus to a subjective
spiritual experience in the individual, not as itself the content of that experience. The spiritualist individual experi-

[margin handwritten note:] Anabaptist.

Emphasis has been upon individual experience of the Spirit, rather than by appropriation of the redemption purchased by Christ.

ences his own conversion and the resultant spiritual glow
rather than Jesus Christ and him crucified; when he bears
his testimony, it is to speak of his new-found peace and
happiness rather than to confess that Jesus Christ is Lord.

A warm inner glow without content.

One of the purposes of the *filioque* clause was to establish an indissoluble connection between the mission of the
Spirit and the work of the incarnate Christ and so to determine the specific character of Christian spirituality. In
severing this connection, enthusiasm leaves itself with no
objective criterion by which to " try the spirits " and thus
exposes itself to the dangers of an unregulated spirituality.
It tends to issue in " varieties of religious experience "
rather than a saving knowledge of God in Christ.

Roman Catholicism has always been the most impla-
cable foe of enthusiasm, because it sees in it, rightly, a
loosening of the historical connection with the incarnation
which is essential to an authentic Christian experience of
the Spirit. In Catholicism itself this connection is maintained primarily by means of institutional continuity; and,
in principle, there can be no objection to this. If the incarnation is really God's decisive deed for the salvation of
the world, and not merely an illustration of a general principle, it must in some way be " extended " if it is to benefit
those who are not immediately contemporaneous with it;
and if, further, the incarnation is taken seriously as the
entrance of God into humanity and his submission to the
conditions of human existence, it would be entirely consistent that the " extension " should involve ordinary historical factors of transmission and communication, and
even an institution. In the Roman Catholic view, the institution of the Church is " the extension of the incarnation." [30] It is through the continuing institution — and its
continuity consists, of course, in the " apostolic succes-

sion " — that the benefits of the incarnation are extended and communicated to men. The claim is justified by appeal to the incarnational principle or " law of incarnation." [31] It is not claimed that institutional continuity by itself is sufficient; the assistance of the Holy Spirit is also essential. But the Holy Spirit, understood as the soul of the Church, is canalized within the historical institution, and institutional continuity remains paramount. In the Roman Catholic view, therefore, the Spirit comes to us, so to speak, horizontally, along the avenue of historical continuity.

Enthusiasts claim that the Spirit comes down directly, and does not use historical media and has no historical content.

This is precisely what enthusiasm rejects. In the enthusiast view the Spirit comes vertically,[32] and is not channeled through media in the horizontal dimension of history. Indeed, there is no mediation of any kind; every man is directly accessible to the Spirit and is not dependent on the mediation of pope, Church, Bible, or sacrament.

The true Protestant position differs from both Catholicism and enthusiasm, in each of which it recognizes a mixture of truth and error. It is at one with enthusiasm in opposing the Catholic attempt to canalize the Spirit in the historically continuous institution, but it agrees with Roman Catholicism in condemning the enthusiast repudiation of all historical mediation. In other words, Protestantism recognizes an element of truth in the Roman Catholic insistence on historical continuity, in accordance with the " law of incarnation "; it also recognizes an element of truth in the enthusiast insistence on the sovereign independence of the Spirit. But it sees error when these truths are isolated from each other and opposed to each other. According to the understanding of the Reformers, the gift of the Spirit is not canalized in the historical body which is continuous with the incarnation, as the Roman Catholics hold (the Spirit, not having been incarnate, cannot be subjected to the "law of incarnation"), but neither is it entirely independent of that body, as the enthusiasts teach (for the Spirit is the Spirit *of* the Incarnate, the Spirit that proceeds from the Father and the Son, *Filioque*).

Enthusiasm presents no serious challenge to Protestantism; for enthusiasm, when it pretends to a Christian experience of the Spirit in independence of the historical tradition, is a patent victim of self-deception. The real issue lies between Protestantism and Roman Catholicism, and it hinges on the question, What precisely is conveyed through the medium of historical continuity? According to the Roman Catholic view, the Church is itself " the extension of the incarnation," but in making this claim the Church tends to arrogate to itself the Lordship of the Spirit, and the incarnation tends to be robbed of its centrality and finality. The true answer is surely that what is extended in the Church is the apostolic *paradosis* of the incarnation. But the incarnation itself can be extended only as the Incarnate himself re-presents himself in answer to the prayer of faith which arises from the apostolic witness. The apostolic testimony provides the sacramental element which the Spirit uses to re-present Christ to men; but it is by the Spirit, who is Lord, and not by any power inherent in the apostles or their successors, that the Christ remembered in the tradition re-presents himself as living Lord and Saviour. In thus correlating the Spirit with the Word (by faith and prayer), the Protestant Church maintains both the centrality of the incarnation and the sovereign Lordship of the Spirit.

IV

The Holy Spirit
and the Word

In the Churches of the Reformation the Holy Spirit is associated pre-eminently with the means of grace, of which the first and foremost is the Word. This association is enshrined in the doctrine of "the inner witness of the Holy Spirit" (*testimonium Spiritus sancti internum*), which is one of the best known elements in the Reformed theological tradition — and also one of the most difficult when it is a question of determining its precise meaning. The controversy that has raged around the inspiration of the Bible during the present century, and is not yet resolved, reflects the persistence of the difficulty. A fresh attempt to elucidate the meaning of the Reformed doctrine concerning the Spirit and the Word may therefore have a contemporary relevance as well as a historical interest.

I

Although the doctrine of the inner witness of the Holy Spirit owes its classical formulation to Calvin, he was not its originator; and it is advisable — indeed, it is essential — to go back to its antecedents in Luther and the Lutheran Reformation. The doctrine early began to assume a rigid aspect under the pressure of interconfessional controversy, and something of this rigidity is already apparent in the thought of Calvin (as it is in that of the later Luther). To grasp the real meaning and intention of the doctrine, we

must look at it as it was before the hardening process had
set in.

The first thing we note is that the context in which the
doctrine of the witness of the Spirit was originally invoked
is not that of authority (in the formal sense), but rather
(as we may call it) that of power. Initially at least, the
authority of Scripture was not an issue between Luther
and Rome. His basic complaint against the Church of his
day was that it treated Scripture only as a means of establishing a historical relation with Christ. In the Roman system Scripture was (and is) a supernaturally authenticated record of the events concerning Jesus Christ; and
the only link that connects that record of the past with
our present is furnished by the continued existence of
the Church. The re-presentation of Christ belongs exclusively to the Church, which, on the basis of the historical
record (and the unwritten tradition) claims the power to
re-present the body and blood of Christ to God in the
sacrifice of the mass. What Luther found was that this
theory, which is plausible enough in its way, is destructive
of the gospel; for the gospel can retain its evangelical
character only if it remains free to come as God's gracious
gift of salvation *to* the Church — which it cannot be if it
is made subject to the power of the Church and dependent
on the operation of the Church. But while the apparatus of
the Church failed him in his quest for the gospel, he made
the discovery that there is a power in the Word that is able
to leap over the gulf of the centuries and speak direct to
the heart of the believer. A living, saving, evangelical faith
can arise only when this power which makes the Word a
living Word is encountered, i.e., only where the Word
proves itself to be the vehicle of the living Christ, " the
cradle in which Christ lies." This power cannot be the

power of the Church — the Church at best can produce a human faith in the veracity of the record (*fides historica*) — it is the power of God himself, the Holy Spirit.

The pragmatic character of Luther's doctrine of the witness of the Spirit is further evidenced by the fact that it is associated primarily with the living word of preaching rather than with the written word of Scripture. It is significant that the Augsburg Confession contains no article on Scripture, but only on the ministry:

" In order that we may obtain this faith [by which we are justified] there has been instituted the ministry of preaching the gospel and dispensing the sacraments. For it is through the Word and the sacraments as means that the Holy Spirit is given, who works faith in those who hear the gospel, when and where it seems good to God." [1]

It is in the gospel in the actuality of being proclaimed (*viva vox evangelii*) that the witness of the Spirit becomes operative to produce assurance of faith.

This emphasis on the preached word as the instrument of the Spirit is found also in some of the classical documents of the Reformed faith. In the Geneva Catechism of 1542, Calvin discusses the question how we are to use the Scriptures to our profit, and he lays it down that it is not sufficient to read them at home; all must listen together to the teaching given by the pastors in the Church, by whose mouth we receive the teaching of the Saviour himself.[2] Similarly, the Second Helvetic Confession, after stating that the canonical Scriptures are the true Word of God, proceeds to affirm that " when that Word is proclaimed to us in the Church today by preachers duly called, we believe it is the word of God itself that is proclaimed." [3] And it is in connection with the preached word that both documents introduce the witness of the Holy

Spirit. The same emphasis is clearly expressed in the familiar words of the Westminster Shorter Catechism:

" The Spirit of God maketh the reading, but especially the preaching, of the Word an effectual means of convincing and converting sinners, and of building them up in holiness and comfort, through faith unto salvation." [4]

In these statements the witness of the Spirit is connected with the effect or efficacy of the Word in use; it has no bearing on the character of the Word antecedent to use; i.e., it carries no implication concerning the canonical authority or the inspiration of Scripture. Luther, as is well known, felt himself free to discriminate within Scripture between those writings which were efficacious to produce faith in Christ and those which were not. Whether this discrimination was well founded, and why he did not press it to what seems to be its logical conclusion, are questions that do not concern us here; the point is mentioned merely to emphasize the fact that for Luther the witness of the Holy Spirit was not a witness concerning Scripture itself, but a witness to Christ, to whom Scripture stands in an instrumental relationship.

Calvin's interest and emphasis in the doctrine are basically the same as Luther's. The testimony of the Spirit is associated primarily with the efficacy of the Word, its power to create faith in the hearts of men: " The Word is the instrument by which the Lord dispenses to believers the illumination of his Spirit." [5] But Calvin introduces a significant addition. The Word is not only the *instrument*, but also the *object* of the Spirit's witness; for the efficacy of the Word is contingent on an acknowledgment of its divine origin, and it is the divine origin of Scripture that is certified by the witness of the Spirit in the first instance:

" As God alone is a sufficient witness to himself in his own Word, so also the Word will never gain credit in the hearts of men, till it be confirmed by the internal testimony of the Spirit. . . . For though it win our reverence by its internal majesty, it never seriously affects us till it is sealed by the Spirit in our hearts. Thus, being illuminated by his power, we believe, not on the strength of our own judgment or that of others, that Scripture is from God; we establish it with a certainty superior to human judgment (just as if we actually beheld the presence of God himself in it) that Scripture came to us, by the ministry of men, from the very mouth of God." [6]

The testimony of the Spirit is equivalent to an affidavit that God is the author of Scripture, and when this is given, Scripture " obtains complete authority with believers, when they are satisfied it came from heaven, as if the living accents of God himself were heard in it." [7] The position is not that men, finding the *message* of Scripture confirmed in their hearts by the testimony of the Holy Spirit, are led to a conviction of its divine origin and authority; but first they receive by the Spirit certification of the authority of Scripture, and then they experience the power of its message.

The thought of Calvin is faithfully reproduced in the well known statement of the Westminster Confession concerning the authority of Scripture: after acknowledging the subordinate role of the Church's testimony and reciting the many marvelous qualities of Scripture " whereby it doth abundantly evidence itself to be the Word of God," the Confession proceeds: " Yet, notwithstanding, our full persuasion and assurance of the infallible truth, and divine authority thereof, is from the inward work of the Holy Spirit, bearing witness by and with the Word in our heart." [8] The testimony of the Spirit, it is clear, is here understood to deliver a formal theological judgment re-

garding the authority of Scripture, and thus, in effect, to
provide a ready-made solution to the difficult problems
that surround the establishment of the canon.

The most difficult of these problems, in the eyes of the
Reformers, arose from the fact that, as a matter of history,
the canon was defined by the Church, and hence it could
be plausibly argued that the authority of Scripture was
in some sense derived from the authority of the Church.
It was a source of particular embarrassment to them that
Augustine, whom they were so eager to claim as an ally,
had in this matter expressed himself in a way which
seemed to play directly into the hands of the enemy: " I
would not believe the gospel, unless I were influenced by
the authority of the Church." [9] Calvin attempts to " de-
Catholicize " Augustine by arguing that he meant only
that " the authority of the Church is an introduction to
prepare us for the faith of the gospel," [10] in the sense that
it is the Church which by the (human) authority of its
testimony directs us to the superior, divine authority of
Scripture, not that the authority of Scripture is essentially
subordinate to that of the Church.[11] How, then, is the authority of Scripture established? Calvin countered the
" Catholic" position with the doctrine of the testimony of
the Holy Spirit, but he was unwittingly led by his polemi-
cal interest to interpret the latter in terms of the former;
i.e., while he denied that the Church could confer formal
authority on Scripture, he ascribed this formal role to the
Holy Spirit, whose testimony he equated with the formal
decision of an ecclesiastical council on the divine origin
and authority of Scripture. Thus Calvin conceives a twofold operation of the Spirit in the Word, which we may
describe (though he does not use these terms) as formal
and material: the Spirit formally attests the authority of

canonical Scripture as a whole, and *then* materially attests its specific content.

The formal aspect of the witness of the Spirit to the Word yields the conviction (one "which requires no reasons . . . but can only be produced by a revelation from heaven") that Scripture came from God, that "we have received it from God's own mouth by the ministry of men." [12] Calvin based the authority of Scripture on its divine origin (which, of course, does not exclude the mediate authorship of men). He developed no theory of inspiration to explain how the Word of God came to prophets and apostles, and to us through them; and he appears to have looked with suspicion on the view that inspiration involves a suspension of the normal faculties. [13] He is content to say that the Spirit of God spoke by the mouth of the prophets, and to rest this conviction on the witness of the same Spirit in our hearts.

But now, does the Holy Spirit furnish us with such a formal attestation of the authority of Scripture, as Calvin suggests? That this question points up the essential weakness of the doctrine, "the Achilles heel," as Strauss called it, is amply proved by the development that took place in the century following Calvin's death. The mounting stress of controversy with Rome soon made it apparent that the inner witness of the Spirit was too vague, elusive, and "subjective" a ground on which to rest the authority of Scripture, and that it was necessary to find something more tangible and "objective" to pit against the historically grounded position of Rome. His successors, therefore, went beyond Calvin, who had been content to leave the fact of inspiration within the realm of Spirit (where it belongs); they proceeded to elaborate a rational or quasi-rational account of the way in which the Word was in-

spired into the prophets and apostles, and thus trans-
formed inspiration into a theory which was capable of
objective verification.

The theory which took shape and acquired the status of
orthodoxy in the Reformed Churches is well known. The
real question which ought to be asked about this theory
is not whether it is plausible in itself, nor whether it is
susceptible of objective verification, but whether it is
compatible with a Christian understanding of the nature
and work of the Holy Spirit. And in order to do this, it is
necessary to examine its historical antecedents.

II

Although there were some elements of novelty about
the theory, or rather the theories, of inspiration advanced
by the theologians of the seventeenth century, they were
for the most part a revival of ideas that had been current
in the Church in the early centuries and that represented
an amalgam of ideas derived from late Judaism and the
religious world of Hellenism.

In the popular religions of ancient Greece, inspiration
was conceived in a " mechanical " sense as a kind of divine
frenzy or ecstasy which came upon the devotees with
overwhelming force, suspending or superseding their normal faculties and impelling them to speech or bodily
movements over which they had no control. The theory
was used to account for the oracles at Delphi and other
places, and sometimes it received a semimaterialistic form
— the source of inspiration was understood to be a vapor
exhaled from the earth, and it was when the priestess, who
sat on a tripod above the chasm, received this vapor into
her body, that she gave forth prophetic utterance. The
theory is set forth by Plutarch thus: " Moreover, the earth

sends forth for men streams of many other potencies, some
of them producing derangements, diseases, or deaths;
others helpful, benignant, and beneficial, as is plain from
the experience of persons who have come upon them. But
the prophetic current and breath is most divine and holy,
whether it issue by itself through the air or come in the
company of running waters; for when it is instilled into
the body, it creates in souls an unaccustomed and unusual
temperament, the peculiarity of which it is hard to describe with exactness, but analogy offers many compari-
sons. It is likely that by warmth and diffusion it opens up
certain passages through which impressions of the future
are transmitted, just as wine, when its fumes rise to the
head, reveals many unusual movements and also words
stored away and unperceived." [14] Plato, who also saw this
divine " madness " as the source of prophecy,[15] gave it a
wider range as the source of poetry as well, and argued
that poetry, no less than prophecy, was the word of God.
Plato says: " For all the good epic poets utter all those
fine poems, not from art, but as inspired and possessed as
the good lyric poets likewise; just as the Corybantian
worshipers do not dance when in their senses, so the lyric
poets do not indite those fine songs in their senses, but
when they have started on the melody and rhythm they
begin to be frantic, and it is under possession — as the
bacchants are possessed and not in their senses, when they
draw honey and milk from the rivers — that the soul of
the lyric poets does the same thing, by their own report. . . . And for this reason God takes away the mind of
these men and uses them as his ministers, just as he does
soothsayers and godly seers, in order that we who hear
them may know that it is not they who utter these words
of great price, when they are out of their wits, but that it

is God himself who speaks and addresses us through them." [16]

These conceptions were familiar to Philo, who imported them into his interpretations of the Old Testament; he associated prophetic inspiration, not with special insight, but with the involuntary utterance of words by a person in a state of ecstasy when his own reasoning faculties are suspended: " For a prophet has no utterance of his own, but all his utterances come from elsewhere, the echoes of another's voice . . . he is the vocal instrument of God smitten and played by his invisible hand." [17]

While little trace of any such theories of inspiration can be found in the Judaism of Palestine and the East, the way was prepared for their reception by developments which took place there too, above all by the shift of interest from the spoken to the written word, and, in consequence, from the prophet to the scribe. It had become axiomatic by the time of the Maccabees that the living word of prophecy had ceased (I Macc. 9:27; cf. Ps. 74:9), but compensation was found in the possession of the written word. The change may be dated roughly from the day on which Ezra the scribe read " the book of the law of Moses " to " all the people gathered together as one man into the street that was before the water gate " (Neh., ch. 8), and from the collection of the corpus of the prophetic writings in the third century. The viva vox of the prophet was replaced by the written word of prophecy (and of the law and " the writings," which by an extension of the idea of prophetic inspiration were also regarded as the work of the Spirit), and the holy book came to be regarded as the standing organ of the Holy Spirit. [18]

With this transference of interest from the primary stage of inspiration (the delivery of the Word by the prophet) to the secondary (the literary preservation and interpretation of the Word by the scribe), a decisive step was taken toward the fusion of Judaic and Hellenistic ideas of inspiration which took place in the thought of Philo. The clearest example of this is to be seen in Philo's famous account of the origin of the Septuagint, in which he says that although the translators had often a choice of Greek synonyms for the Hebrew words of the original, "they prophesied like ecstatics, not one one way and another another, but all the same names and words, as if an invisible teacher dictated to each one of them." [19] Here inspiration has become predominantly *verbal* inspiration, i.e., the supply of words to speakers and, more especially, to writers, independently of their own volition.

This conception was first introduced into Christian thought by some of the apologists of the second century, who applied it to the Old Testament prophets; both Justin Martyr and Athenagoras liken them to musical instruments in the hands of a divine player. The theory did not receive dogmatic sanction, and interest in the question of inspiration tended to diminish as the authority of Scripture came to be overshadowed by the authority of the Church. But it was inevitably revived when the Reformation asserted the authority of Scripture alone (*sola Scriptura*) and opposed it to the authority of the Church. So far as the Reformers themselves are concerned, they realized that Scripture could have authority in the Church and over the Church only if its authority stemmed from that same source from which the Church derived its existence. This is what they tried to express in their different ways, Luther by saying that the Bible contains Christ like a cradle, Calvin even more strongly with his doctrine that none but the Spirit of Christ can disclose and communi-

cate the message of the Bible. There was no thought in
their minds of framing a rational theory to support the
authority of Scripture; rather, their meaning was that
the ground of the authority of Scripture belongs within the
area of its content and can be discovered only in an act
of faith and prayer. It was the pressure of continuing controversy with Rome, as has been already mentioned, that
led the successors of the Reformers to give their doctrine
of the witness of the Holy Spirit the more concrete and
rational form of a theory of inspiration. The great strength
of the Roman position rested in its claims, which were
alleged to be historically verifiable, to direct divine institution and divinely guaranteed immunity from error. The
ancient theory of inspiration was invoked, because it
seemed to lend to Scripture a superior title to precisely
these two things: the conception of the human writers as
passive instruments in the hands of the Spirit gave to
Scripture the virtual status of a divine holograph and imparted a divine sanction to its every word. The only real
innovation that was made by the theologians of the post-
Reformation era (apart from their elaborate, scholastic
analyses of the act of inspiration) was the equation of
verbal inspiredness with verbal inerrancy. This notion has
often been regarded as the essence of inspiration, and as
such it has figured prominently in modern controversy;
yet it is, in fact, a product — a characteristic product — of
the seventeenth century, derived in part from the legalistic
temper of the age and in part from the desire to outdo the
Roman claims for the Church. These claims, though lofty,
were seriously weakened by the abundant historical records of the Church's errancy, and could not compete with
those of a document, which, by virtue of its origin, possessed the authority of divine law in its minutest particular.

III

While the collapse of the " orthodox " theory of inspiration came about primarily through the advent of literary
and historical criticism and the factual demonstration of
the errancy of the Biblical writers, the real argument
against it is to be found in the distorted conception of the
nature and work of the Holy Spirit, which it implies. If
I attempt to pursue the root of the error in this direction,
it may help to point the way to a truer understanding of
the meaning of the Spirit in the Word. Let me make three
critical observations:

1. In their determination to assert the authority of Scripture over the Church, in opposition to the Roman doctrine,
the theologians of the post-Reformation period were (unwittingly) led to set up a false antithesis between the
Scripture and the Church. The Roman doctrine, which
makes Scripture (like tradition) a divine instrument in the
hands of the authoritative Church, derives a certain plaus-
ibility from the historical fact that the Church was in existence before Scripture (at least the New Testament) and
that it was the Church which collected the writings of the
New Testament and made them canonical. The inference
drawn by some Roman controversialists, that the authority
of Scripture is subordinate to the authority of the Church,
presented no difficulty to the Reformers, since it was easy
to show that in the act of canonization the Church did
not pretend to *confer* authority on Scripture, but, on the
contrary, acknowledged the authority of Scripture over
itself; [20] had the Church felt itself to be possessed of the
authority that the Romans claim for it, it is difficult to see
why it should have felt any need to set up a canon of
Scripture.[21] Nevertheless, it was a patent embarrassment to

the Reformers that the Church should play even a subordinate role in this matter, and they strove to eliminate it
completely by establishing the authority of Scripture on a
ground with which the Church had nothing to do. The
first step was taken by Calvin, as we saw; the real meaning of his teaching is made plain in the *Confession* of La
Rochelle, where it is expressly stated that the canonicity
of the canonical books is an immediate deliverance of the
Holy Spirit, independent of the historical judgment of the
Church.[22]

Now, the idea that a formal distinction like that of
canonical and apocryphal can be derived from "the interior witness and persuasion of the Holy Spirit" without
regard to exterior data like the decision of the Church or
the criteria which it took into account in reaching its decision, must be dismissed as a pious delusion. Can it be
seriously maintained that the inner witness of the Spirit is
sufficient to inform us (for example) that the book of The
Proverbs is of divine origin and therefore to be received as
authoritative, while the book of The Wisdom of Solomon,
"not being of divine inspiration" is "of no authority in
the Church of God, nor to be any otherwise approved, or
made use of, than other human writings"? [23] Moreover,
the underlying assumption that the testimony of the Spirit
will coincide with the ecclesiastical definition of the canon
and render it superfluous is not borne out by experience.
The truth is, as is well known, that those who rely exclusively on the inner witness of the Spirit have frequently
found themselves in conflict with the ecclesiastical definition. In addition to Luther, whose discriminatory attitude to the canonical New Testament is well known, the
case of Bunyan may be mentioned. Having found great
comfort in the text, "Look at the generations of old, and

see; did ever any trust in the Lord and was confounded? " he sought for it in canonical Scripture, but in vain. Later, he writes, " Casting my eye upon the Apocrypha books, I found it in Ecclesiasticus, chapter two, verse ten. This at first did somewhat daunt me, because it was not in those texts that we call holy and canonical: yet as this sentence was the sum and substance of many of the promises, it was my duty to take the comfort of it. And I bless God for that word, for it was good to me. That word doth still ofttimes shine before my face." [24]

There was here an evident failure to realize that while the authority of canonical Scripture is not conferred upon it by the Church, it is inseparably bound up with the testimony of the Church. The definition of the canon was, in the last analysis, an act of faith on the part of the Church, and canonical authority has meaning only in relation to the faith of the Church. In other words, Scripture is essentially what it is *in* the Church. This is the truth that the Reformers tended to forget when they asserted the authority of Scripture *over* the Church in opposition to the Roman Catholic doctrine which set Scripture *under* the Church. They did, indeed, recognize it when they approached it from the other side — they defined the Church as the sphere in which Scripture is operative; i.e., it is Scripture that makes the Church the Church. They did not take sufficient account of the complementary truth that it is in the Church that Scripture is Scripture. By their unnatural severance of the authority of Scripture from its natural context in the faith of the Church and their attempt to make it dependent exclusively on the inner witness of the Spirit, they laid the foundation for the subsequent development of a distorted conception of the operation of the Spirit and, in consequence, a distorted conception of the nature and scope of Scripture.

2. The refusal to accept the historical testimony of the Church's faith as the external correlate or counterpart of the inner witness of the Holy Spirit left the latter vulnerable to the charge of subjectivism, and it was to escape this charge that appeal was made to the quality of Scripture itself, which was considered to furnish objective evidence of its having been divinely inspired. But the equation of inspiration with inerrancy reflects a conception of spirit that belongs to the mantic cults of ancient Greece rather than to the faith of the New Testament.[25] The spirit whose operation in the Biblical writers was analyzed into the *impulsus ad scribendum*, the *suggestio rerum*, and the *suggestio verborum*, is the spirit of the Delphic oracle, not the Spirit of Christ.

There was in this a manifest failure to practice that "discrimination of spirits," on which the New Testament lays emphasis (I Cor. 12:10), and for which it offers certain tests (John 15:26; I Cor. 12:3; I John 4:1 ff.). Two of these may be applied. (*a*) If it be accepted as the primary test that the Holy Spirit is the Spirit that bears witness to Christ and to the truth that came by him, the orthodox doctrine of inspiration posits a spirit with a much wider range of operation. When it was taught, as the theory required, that every single matter in Scripture, even though it lay within the natural knowledge of the writer, was written "at the special suggestion, inspiration, and dictation of the Holy Spirit" (Quenstedt); when it was taught (to give the classic example) that Paul wrote to Timothy about the cloak he left at Troas (II Tim. 4:13), not because he remembered it, but because he was divinely inspired to do so, not even the most rigid advocates of the theory could maintain that such matters came within the

scope of the purpose assigned to Scripture in the selfsame
epistle, viz., that of " instructing us for salvation through
faith in Christ Jesus" (II Tim. 3:15). The theory made
inspiration much more extensive than revelation, as some
of its exponents did not hesitate to acknowledge, unaware
that by so doing they were in effect confessing to having
invoked a conception of spirit which could not, except in
an arbitrary way, be identified with the Spirit of the
Father and the Son. (b) It is pertinent to ask whether the
mode of operation ascribed to the Spirit in the theory does
not cast suspicion upon its identity with the Spirit of
Christ. Does the experience of the " inspired " writers not
show a closer affinity with possession by evil spirits? The
authors of the orthodox theory of inspiration, like their
precursors in the Early Church, appear to have proceeded
on the assumption that possession by spirits, both good
and evil, conforms to the same pattern. But it is just this
assumption that Paul is mainly concerned to refute in his
long discussion of " spirituals " in I Corinthians. He introduces the theme by pointing a contrast between pagan
and Christian conceptions of spirituality: as pagans, he
reminds them, they were victims of an involuntary seduc-
tion or a blind infatuation; they had now to learn that the
presence of the Spirit of Christ is marked by an articulate
confession of faith in him (ch. 12:1–3). The grave threat
to the integrity of the faith which Paul evidently saw in
the introduction of pagan notions of spirituality into the
Christian Church has been recognized more than once on
its recurrence in history. It was not recognized that the inspiration ascribed to the Biblical writers in the orthodox
theory belongs to the pagan rather than to the Christian
type of experience.

   3. The conception of spirit and spiritual operation im-

plied in the theory of inspiration is hard to reconcile with
the personality of the Holy Spirit. The personality of the
Holy Spirit is an essential element of Trinitarian doctrine;
but there was nothing very personal about the activity
of the Spirit (as it was conceived) in the Biblical writers
— it came, in fact, to be generally characterized as mechanical — nor about the faith associated with it, which
involved acceptance of a large assortment of propositional
statements. The real ground of the doctrine of the personality of the Holy Spirit is the relation of the Spirit to
Christ. The Spirit is another (*allos*) than Christ; yet the
presence (as *parakletos*) of the Spirit is not other than
the presence of Christ (John 14:16); for it is precisely the
function of the Spirit to re-present Christ (John 16:14),
and it is the living Christ himself who is present in the
Spirit (John 14:18). There is no such thing as an experience of the presence of the Spirit distinct from the presence of Christ; [26] the Christian experience is an experience
of the presence of Christ in the Spirit, and as such it is a
personal experience, an encounter with One who is *Kyrios*.
The original intention of the Reformers' doctrine of the
testimony of the Holy Spirit was to affirm that Christian
faith means nothing less than personal experience of the
living Christ, and that it is the function of Scripture to
serve as means to that end. In other words, they taught,
as they had found, that the written testimony of prophets
and apostles to Christ can really lead men beyond itself to
an encounter with Christ himself, and they could account
for this power only by ascribing it to the Spirit of the living Christ, confirming the testimony of the Word in men's
hearts. But when Calvin made the testimony of the Spirit
in the Word to Christ contingent on a testimony of the
Spirit *to* the Word, i.e., to its divine authorship, he ob-

scured the essentially personal character of faith and opened the door to the subsequent development of the theory of inspiration, in which the obscurity became total. The main insight of the Reformation was that faith is a personal relation with God in Christ through the Holy Spirit, and that it is the function of Church, Bible, sacraments, etc., to serve as means to this end. Whenever any of these mediating factors is elevated to a position that obscures the end it serves, whenever it interposes itself between faith and its true object, faith becomes depersonalized, and it is time to protest. The Reformers were able to break through the Roman Catholic front at the point of the Word, which they found the most potent weapon against all false absolutes. The subsequent development of the theory of inspiration meant the betrayal of the Reformation precisely at the point of its decisive break-through and a relapse into the obtrusion of impersonal authorities against which its basic protest had been directed.

IV

What, then, in the light of these critical observations, are we to say of the positive significance of the doctrine of the Spirit in the Word? I believe it will be sufficient to say that in order to understand this doctrine aright, it is essential to keep two things in view, which I would describe summarily as content and context.

For the Reformers, as we have seen, the testimony of the Holy Spirit was related primarily to the efficacy of the Word, i.e., to the power of its content to communicate itself as living reality to the hearer or reader. They were not interested in the form in which this content was to be found in Scripture, because its power to communicate itself proved it to be essentially incommensurable with any form. When, for example, in Luther's experience the word of justification by faith in Rom. 1:17 came alive, so to speak, and leaped from the printed page and seized him as Jacob was seized by that ghostly wrestler at the ford Jabbok, it was not of the verbal inerrancy of the text or the inspiration of its writer or even of its divine origin that he thought, but of the power of the Spirit, through this word, to communicate the gospel of Christ to him effectually. It was to the experience of readers of the Bible rather than to that of its writers that the witness of the Spirit was related.

It was not, however, the intensity or vitality of the experience that registered the presence of the Spirit. This is the romantic misunderstanding to which some have been led in reaction against mechanical theories of inspiration. Its most famous statement was given by Coleridge: "Whatever *finds* me, bears witness for itself that it has proceeded from a Holy Spirit." [27] It is present also in the thought of some more recent theologians who seek to ground the inspiration of Scripture on the "appeal it makes to the heart and conscience." [28] There is, of course, an element of truth in this position. It is certain that the witness of the Holy Spirit is not likely to be known without such a warming of the heart. But when the whole case is made to rest on the quality of the experience; when, for example, it is said that "The Bible is inspired because it is inspiring," [29] we are in danger of subjectivism, because we have no reason why the experience that comes through reading the Bible should be ascribed to the Holy Spirit any more than other inspiring experiences. The appeal of Scripture should not be confused with the emotional quality of the experience which it evokes; it is its specific content that is the decisive factor.[30]

If we ask what precisely the appeal of Scripture is, the New Testament leaves us in no doubt of the answer. The appeal of Scripture is the appeal of its testimony to Jesus Christ and the gospel of God which is the finished work of his incarnate life. The author of the Fourth Gospel speaks for all the writers of Scripture when he says of his own work: " These are written, that ye might believe that Jesus is the Christ, the Son of God; and that believing ye might have life through his name " (John 20:31). In other words, the Scriptures were not written to draw attention to themselves, and their appeal does not arise from any property in themselves. Their appeal proceeds from Him to whom they bear witness, and they are only the medium or vehicle of it, as Paul says of the preaching of the apostles: " We are ambassadors for Christ, God making his appeal through us " (II Cor. 5:20).

To use a paradox, the content of Scripture is not (and cannot be) " contained " in Scripture. Scripture stands to its " content " in the relation of testimony to a reality that transcends itself. This must be kept in view if the other aspects of Scripture are to be seen in their true perspective. Thus Scripture also presents the aspect of a record of facts, and since its testimony is conveyed through this record, it is easy to suppose that the right response to the testimony consists in acceptance of the record. How, it is asked, could anything be conveyed to us through Scripture at all — or anything except airy fancies — unless the veracity of the record could be relied on? Clearly there is point to the question. If the veracity of the record could be seriously impugned — if, to give the stock example, it could be proved that Jesus never lived and that the Gospel records of his life were completely fictitious, that would

be an end of the whole matter. But, on the other hand, if
the veracity of the record is insisted on as a condition (or
consequence) of the validity of the reality to which it
bears testimony, this is to forget that *this* reality is incommensurable with the most perfect record that could be
imagined. It is this incommensurability which the author
of the Fourth Gospel expresses when he writes: "There
are also many other things which Jesus did; were every
one of them to be written, I suppose that the world itself
could not contain the books that would be written" (John
21:25). And it was the converse of it that Kierkegaard had
in mind when he suggested that the truth would stand
even if the record were reduced to minimal proportions:
"If the contemporary generation had left behind them
nothing but the words, 'We have believed that in such
and such a year God appeared among us in the humble
figure of a servant, that he lived and taught in our com-
munity, and finally died,' it would be more than enough." [31]
This, of course, is an extreme statement, but it is an extreme statement of the truth that the gospel, to which
Scripture bears testimony, is not authenticated by the nature and extent of the record in which the testimony is
presented. "Let God be true, but every man a liar"
(Rom. 3:4).

Much of the difficulty that is felt in this matter arises
from failure to consider Scripture in its context. The problem of inspiration has often been discussed as if Scripture
were the only means through which the gospel is conveyed, and as if it existed in a vacuum. If we make this assumption, the argument that the veracity of the record is a
necessary condition, or implicate, of the validity of the
testimony, carries considerable force. But the assumption
is false; for Scripture does not stand alone. Despite the

sola Scriptura of Luther and the orthodox doctrine of the *sufficiency* of Scripture (both of which had their valid meaning), *Scriptura* has never been *sola,* nor has it ever been treated as sufficient. The means of grace, as the Westminster Standards attest, are the Word, sacraments, and prayer. If this does not mean that the Word, or either of the others by itself, is less than sufficient to convey the fullness of the gospel, I do not know what it can mean. But even if we confine our attention to Scripture alone, it must be remembered that Scripture has always been what it is in the Church, and its testimony has always been accompanied by the testimony of the Church. The relation between them is twofold: The testimony of the Church is a response to the testimony of Scripture, which is prior to it; in the testimony of the Church the testimony of Scripture is heard and repeated. But it is also through the testimony of the Church that the testimony of Scripture is brought out. The thought that it can come to a living, personal relation with the reality attested in Scripture would not (normally) suggest itself to the reader apart from the testimony of the Church's faith. This is not to say that it is the Church that makes the Word effectual. The Word becomes effectual by the testimony of the Holy Spirit — but it is only within the context of the Church's faith that its efficacy is known.

It was necessary at the Reformation to assert the doctrine of the Spirit in the Word in opposition to the Roman Catholic doctrine of the Spirit in the Church, but the reason for this was, paradoxically, that there can be no real opposition between them; for the Spirit is in the Church only when it is a Church of the Word, and the Spirit is in the Word only when it is the Word in the Church. It is the Church that is defined as the communion of the Holy

Spirit. The Reformers had no wish to deny this. Their intention was merely to emphasize that the Church truly participates in the Holy Spirit when, through the testimony of the Word, it is united in faith and obedience to its Lord. Luther said the Word is the cradle in which Christ lies; we may also say that the Church is the nursery in which the cradle lies. To isolate the doctrine of the Spirit in the Word from its context in the faith of the Church is to put asunder what God has joined together.

To sum up, the testimony of the Spirit in the Word is registered, not in any properties of the Scriptural record, but where the Church receives the testimony of the Word and repeats it in the testimony of its own faith. It occurs, so to speak, at the point where the testimony of Scripture and the testimony of the Church converge. But this is a point outside and above themselves, a point that they can reach only by overreaching themselves. This point is the presence of the living Lord in the power of his finished work. The testimony of Scripture and the testimony of the Church are instrumental to it; but they cannot effect it — least of all by the advancement of exalted claims on behalf of either of them. The doctrine of the testimony of the Holy Spirit makes all such claims redundant; for it means that, despite the frailty and fallibility of the Church, despite the errancy of Scripture, nevertheless the living Lord makes himself known to us through their testimony. They are *means* of grace; but the grace is that of the Lord Jesus Christ, which proceeds from the love of God and is imparted to us in the communion of the Holy Spirit.

V

The Holy Spirit
and the Human Spirit

The problem of the relation between the Holy Spirit and the human spirit is one that has been curiously neglected in the main stream of Christian theology. Throughout the greater part of its history, Christian theology has been chiefly concerned with the doctrine of the Holy Spirit, the Spirit "who proceeds from the Father and the Son," and in this it has been faithful to the emphasis of the New Testament; it has shown little interest in the question how this Spirit is related in essence and operation to the spirit that is in man, and in this too it has followed the example of the New Testament. Yet the New Testament recognizes that man is a being endowed with spirit, and the question was bound to arise (if only because they bear the same name) how the divine Spirit is related to the human.

I

The question first arose when the Christian faith spread beyond the confines of Judaism and entered the world of Greek culture, where it encountered a lofty view of the significance and capacity of the human spirit (if not always under that name). The conception of spirit, which may be described as one of the most characteristic products of the Greek genius, is discernible in germ in the thought of Heraclitus [1] and receives its classical expression in Plato. As the principle of man's self-transcendence, or awareness of transcendent reality, spirit manifests itself in the form of longing or aspiration, that *eros,* or love of the perfect and heavenly beauty, which is described in Plato's *Symposium.* The prevalence of this type of thought seemed to present an ideal opportunity for a theology of correlation, and despite protests by isolated figures, like Tertullian, who held that there could be no traffic between Athens and Jerusalem, the theologians of the Early Church, for the most part, sought to come to terms with pagan philosophy by interpreting the *eros* of the human spirit as an aspiration after that fulfillment which is realized in the gift of the divine Spirit. The principal exponent of this approach in the ancient Church was, of course, Augustine, for whom the unrestful striving which he found at the core of existence is the index of an ontological orientation of the creature toward the Creator: "Thou has made us for thyself, and our hearts are restless till they find their rest in thee"; [2] and this implies the presence in man of a principle or capacity for self-transcendence: "Man was so created that by means of that in him which transcends (*praecellit*) he should attain to that which transcends all things, that is the true and best and only God." [3] This theology of correlation came to its full flower in medieval Scholasticism, where the doctrine of man was dominated by the motif of aspiration. To Aquinas, for example, the essence of all intelligent creatures is their tendency to seek their beatitude and chief end in God, and though he does not do so, it is natural to ascribe the desire of the finite for the infinite to the human spirit. [4] The appeal of this type of correlation theology is obvious, and its persistence, both in Roman Catholicism and elsewhere, is easy to understand. [5] Echoes of it are to be heard even in the young Luther; in his *Exposition of the Magnificat*

(1521), Luther describes the spirit as "the highest, deepest, noblest part of man, by which he is able to grasp incomprehensible, invisible, and eternal things."[6]

It soon came to be felt, however, that such a view could not be held in conjunction with the main emphasis of the Reformation. The sufficiency of grace alone left no need of correlation with anything on the part of man, but implied rather his total incapacity. Faith in the Holy Spirit, according to Luther's famous words in his *Smaller Catechism,* means: "I believe that I cannot by my own reason or power believe in Jesus Christ my Lord or come to him; but the Holy Spirit has called me through the gospel, enlightened me with his gifts, sanctified and preserved me in the true faith."[7] Here no mention is made of the human spirit, and its role, if any could be assigned to it, would be merely to form the area or sphere in which the Holy Spirit comes to operate, as, indeed, Luther suggests in the sequel to the passage cited above from the *Exposition of the Magnificat:* The spirit, he says, unlike the soul which is illumined by the light of reason, has no light of its own; it is a dark room, like the holy of holies in the Temple, "where God dwells in the darkness of faith, without light."[8] But it is difficult to see why this conception should bear the name of spirit, since it is entirely passive and lacking in the dynamic movement that is characteristic of spirit. The Reformers rapidly lost interest in the human spirit altogether, and for an obvious reason: When the full force of their new apprehension of the gospel was deployed theologically, it seemed to obliterate the spirit of man and reduce him to the level of an inanimate object like a stone or a tree.[9] Calvin recognized the significance of the human spirit and sought to give it a place in his thought. In the opening chapters of the *Institutes,* he seems to be laying

the foundation for a theology of correlation. Calvin saw
in the existence (and persistence) of idolatry a proof that
some sense of deity is inscribed on every human heart.
Man's true felicity and the end for which he is born and
lives is the knowledge of God: "thus the chief operation
of the soul is to aspire after it." [10] But it soon becomes clear
that this is predicable only of unfallen man; in fallen, sinful man this aspiration of the spirit has become perverted
and corrupted, and when man is brought to the real knowledge of God through his Word and Spirit, the human spirit
plays no significant part. The knowledge of God is made to
depend so exclusively on the downreach of the divine
Spirit that any movement of upreach on the part of the
human spirit can be construed only as an attempt to by-
pass it.[11] The consequence was that the spirit of man was
not brought into a positive relation with the Spirit of
God in faith; and man was to all intents and purposes
"de-spirited." In theological anthropology the preference
was decidedly for dichotomy, and spirit received only a
grudging recognition as an aspect or faculty of the soul;
Calvin never speaks of the spirit of man, but always of the
soul or mind, except where he is under exegetical necessity, as in I Cor. 2:11. His comment on that passage is:
"Observe that here the spirit of man is taken for the soul
in which the intellectual power, as they call it, resides."
But this spirit is spirit in name only, for it lacks the distinctive movement of spirit, viz., aspiration: "Man," says
Calvin, "is so enslaved by sin as to be of his own nature
incapable of an effort, or even an aspiration, toward that
which is good." [12] Human aspiration, accordingly, played
no part in the encounter with divine grace; the role of the
human spirit in this encounter is one of complete passivity; for man is spiritually dead, until he is quickened

and renewed by the Holy Spirit.[13]

The Reformers felt themselves forced to this conclusion (to the difficulties of which they were not entirely insensitive) by their understanding of the gospel. The sovereignty and sufficiency of grace left no room for human effort or even for human aspiration. The *Agape* motif dominated the picture so completely, that *eros* was eliminated altogether.

Such was the classical pattern of the Lutheran and Reformed theologies, and it is vigorously upheld in some of their contemporary expressions. Someone has put it in epigrammatic form: " God is everything; man is nothing." And though this is, no doubt, a caricature, like most epigrams, at least no one needs to ask what it is a caricature of. But, smile at it as we may, how can we avoid it if we follow the logic of the gospel? If we start out from the initiative of God, the sufficiency of grace, the exclusiveness of *Agape*-love, it seems difficult to resist the conclusion that man's part in the affair is one of sheer passivity.

II

The Church has wrestled with this problem under different forms at different times in its history. The controversy between Augustine and Pelagius in the fifth century, the struggle between Calvinists and Arminians in the seventeenth century, the disputes of recent decades over the questions of natural theology and the image of God, all revolve around the same problem, viz., What role, if any, can be assigned to man in the encounter with the gospel that will not conflict with the sovereignty of grace and at the same time conserve man's essential humanity? It is this same problem that we pose, when we ask, What is the relation between the Spirit of God and the spirit of man?

And it seems to me that in approaching the problem from this angle, and in opening up this somewhat neglected aspect of it, we may hope to avoid the impasse in which discussion of the problem in its traditional forms is all too likely to end.

The theology of the Reformation, as I have said, implies the virtual elimination of the human spirit as a factor in man's encounter with the gospel. There are three grounds, it seems to me, on which this position is open to question: They may be described as philosophical, exegetical, and theological, respectively.

1. If it be argued that philosophical objections are incompetent in a theological court, the answer is that theology and philosophy have a common point of interest in the nature of man, and a radical contradiction between them at this point would be intolerable. Indeed, this is pretty much what happened. The theological conception of a condition in which man is " altogether passive " [14] and the human spirit plays no active part, was found, when it was examined philosophically and psychologically, to be quite untenable. Man cannot be deprived of active spirit without ceasing to be man. The development of the philosophy of spirit in post-Kantian idealism, originating in Germany, may be interpreted historically as a revolt against the suppression of the spirit in Protestant theology; for it was in its initial intention an affirmation, or re-affirmation, of the human spirit. This was sometimes obscured behind the metaphysical constructions erected upon it, according to which the spirit in man was interpreted as an immanence of the Holy Spirit, as in Fichte, who describes it as " an affinity with the supersensible world which is present in man naturally and independently of the teaching of Jesus," [15] or as a moment in the

self-realization of the absolute spirit, as in Hegel. It comes out more clearly in the phenomenological approach of recent thinkers like Max Scheler, for whom spirit is the source of man's unique ability " to elevate himself above himself as a living being and, as it were, from a center beyond the spatiotemporal world, to make everything, including himself, an object of his knowledge." [16] As the capacity for self-transcendence, the impulse to reach up to and aspire after the universal and the eternal, spirit is seen as the distinctive feature of man; it is that which distinguishes him from all other creatures; it is the secret of that creativity which he alone of all intelligent beings has evinced.[17]

> ". . . unless above himself he can
> Erect himself, how poor a thing is man."

The significance of this conception of spirit for the Christian understanding of man was first perceived by Kierkegaard, and it is doubtless to his influence that we may ascribe its current adoption in Christian anthropology. The concept of spirit plays a decisive part in the thought of Niebuhr, for whom it signifies that, while man is a child of nature, he also " stands outside nature, life, himself, his reason, and the world." [18] As such, spirit is the distinctive characteristic of man and the secret both of his grandeur and of his misery. It stands for the fact, as it has been put by another writer,[19] that man is permanently maladjusted to his environment, and is impelled to reach out to the transcendent. " The essential homelessness of the human spirit is the ground of all religion; for the self which stands outside itself and the world cannot find the meaning of life in itself or the world." [20] In similar terms, Emil Brunner finds the essence of spirit in its relation to "something beyond the existing sphere," to that which is meaningful, valid, normative; "spirit, in contradisti ..ion from that which is merely functional and psychical, can only be understood as something 'transcending' the ordinary level, aspiring after something 'beyond the self,' an original actuality." [21] Brunner contends that the true transcendence of the human spirit can be understood only "from above," i.e., from its relation to the divine Spirit, and this is true, but it does not alter the fact that the element of transcendence as such discloses itself to a view of spirit "from below"; and one specific aspect of it, viz., the relation of spirit to transcendent meaning, has been present in the tradition of idealistic philosophy from Plato. Professor George F. Thomas gives a prominent place to this factor in his phenomenological analysis of spirit:

"The spiritual activity of an individual is that which is directed towards *universal* truth and value. It is by his identification of himself with the universal that a person enters the spiritual life. The reason for this lies in that capacity for 'self-transcendence' which is the glory of mind. The most profound thing in Plato's theory of love is his statement that it indicates at once a defect of being on the part of the soul and an aspiration to overcome that defect by seeking to possess the perfection it lacks. Similarly the Scholastics hold that, though the human soul is finite, it has an aspiration that can be filled with nothing short of the infinite. Spirit involves a kind of union of the individual with the universal." [22]

There can, of course, be no question of an equation of Platonism and Christianity. As Thomas points out, decisive consequences follow from the fact that " in Plato's theory the universal is impersonal and abstract, whereas in the Christian theory it is personal and concrete." Yet it remains true, both appear to be at one in a view of "the spirit of man that goeth upward" (Eccl. 3:21).

2. If contemporary Christian anthropology shows an
affinity with, and a hospitable attitude toward, the conception of spirit that was recovered by idealistic philosophy, it may well be because of a feeling that this conception does fuller justice to the Biblical conception of spirit
than the scheme of orthodox soteriology accorded to it.
While orthodoxy, as we have seen, tended to suggest that
the spirit of man is a negligible factor prior to his encounter with the gospel and the quickening influence of the
Spirit of grace, dispassionate exegetical study would seem
to indicate that the Bible attaches considerable importance
to the fact that man as God's creature is a being endowed
with spirit.

At the most primitive level, spirit was conceived as the
breath of life and was not distinguished from the soul.
This distinction appears later, but it was never so sharply
drawn as in Greek thought; for since the very life of man,
like that of all creatures, derives from God and is continually dependent upon him, there was no room for a
concept of the soul as a purely immanent principle of life.
Life had always a transcendent, Godward reference. When
the concept of spirit came to be more clearly distinguished
from that of soul, it was to express the consciousness of
man's relation to God rather than the fact. I think Niebuhr
overstresses the distinction in a Greek direction when he
says that *ruach* gradually became " the more specific
designation of man's organ of relation to God, in distinction to *nephesh* which achieves a connotation identical
with ' soul ' or *psyche,* or the life principle in man "; [23]
this is not borne out by the evidence of the Old Testament, which seems rather to support the view that the
essential *differentia* of *ruach* is consciousness. Eichrodt
describes *ruach* as " the organ of mental life, the center of

the thoughts, purposes and moods " [24]; like all that is in man, it is derived from God (Job 32:8), but it is not intrinsically or exclusively directed toward God. Bultmann's analysis of the meaning of *pneuma* in the Pauline anthropology yields much the same result; he finds that when it denotes a special aspect of man (which is not always the case), it is the conscious or cognitive aspect, corresponding to the *nous* of Greek psychology, and in some places it approximates to the modern conception of self-consciousness.[25]

This, however, does not reduce spirit to a purely immanental conception or strip it of its transcendent reference. On the contrary, it is precisely the spirit that furnishes the key to the Biblical understanding of man's self-transcendence; it is spirit that keeps the relation between God and man essentially free and personal. This may best be seen if we consider two apparently contradictory emphases in the Biblical delineation of the relation.

On the one hand, there is, as we have already noticed, a strong emphasis on the dependence of man's life (and of all life) on the divine Spirit. This is often expressed in terms that suggest that the Spirit of God is immanent in man as the principle of his life, and such language has led some theologians to deny the existence of a distinct human spirit. It is a question, however, whether this position, which stresses the absolute dependence of man on God, does not tend to conflict with the other Biblical emphasis on the discontinuity of man and God. It is true, defenders of the dichotomous position have argued that to admit a created spirit in addition to the Creator Spirit would be to posit an element common to God and man and so to blur the radical distinction between them. But this danger seems as likely to arise from the view of an immanence of

the Spirit of God in man, which could be misused to form
a pantheistic or mystical cosmology in which the participation of the creatures in the divine Spirit would serve
as basis for a natural unity of the Creator and the creature.
In the Old Testament, as Eichrodt points out, the idea of
the Spirit is employed precisely to guard against this danger, as well as to stress the absolute dependence of the
creature on the Creator, who is free at any moment to re-
voke the gracious gift of his Spirit. Eichrodt refers to the
story of Gen. 6:1–4, where the true relation of man to
God is set in dramatic contrast to the mythological conception of a race of semi-divine beings: "In contrast to
heathen thought, with its numerous traditions of races of
heroes, the same material is employed here to demonstrate
in an unmistakable manner the unbridgeable gulf which
separates the creature from the eternal God." [26]

It is this paradoxical combination of emphases that provides the key to the essential meaning of spirit in Scripture, and explains the eventual recognition of the human
spirit in Biblical thought. While the powerful sense of the
dependence of all creaturely existence on God sometimes
led to the use of language that equated vitality with direct
participation in the divine Spirit and left no room for a
human spirit, it came to be realized that man's unique
ability to acknowledge his relation to the divine Spirit
implies his ability to encounter spirit in its own medium,
so to speak, and this is intelligible only in terms of his
endowment with created spirit. Created spirit is not to be
thought of as a fragment of the Spirit of God or of some
continuous element in which God and man participate
together, but rather as the *image* of the divine Spirit; if we
were to draw a parallel between the two creation narratives in Genesis, the inbreathing of the divine breath or

Spirit in Gen. 2:7 (J) would correspond to the creation of
man in the divine image in Gen. 1:27 (P).[27] The point is
that a distinction must be observed between man's existen-
tial *dependence* on God, which he shares with all living
creatures and which applies to him as an " ensouled body,"
and man's personal *relation* to God, which can be realized
only at the level of spirit. The difference is that man's creaturely dependence on God is inherent in the structure of
his being; his relation to God at the level of spirit involves
his free and conscious act. At the same time, however,
the freedom of the spirit in man must not be separated
from the structure of the soul; for it is only in the light of
the relation between them that we can understand the
nature of creaturely freedom, which is always structured
freedom. That is to say, the spirit of man, as the spirit of
the creature whom God created for himself, has the true
goal of its aspiration in God; yet, as spirit is free, its direction to God appears, in a phenomenological view, as only
one possibility. As Bultmann says, with reference to the
Pauline doctrine: " The goal of the direction is not determined in the ontological structure of being directed;
but this structure (which is, of course, for Paul a gift of
the Creator of life) yields the possibility of a choice of
goals, a decision for good or evil, for or against God." [28] In
other words, man's relation to God, which corresponds to
the structure of his being as God's creature, can be realized only by the free act of the human spirit. Thus the
human spirit is merely the index of man's self-transcendence, i.e., his ability to elevate himself above himself (as
Scheler puts it); but this does not of itself relate him to
God — it may lead him to an " encounter with nothing-
ness." [29] Yet the human spirit is the organ of his encounter
with the Spirit of God. This appears to be the teaching of

Paul, as we find it in his most extended treatment of the theme in I Cor., ch. 2. The presence of a human spirit in man does not of itself relate him to the Spirit of God; for the Spirit of God is only to be received as his gift. Yet the analogy drawn between the human spirit as the capacity for self-transcendence (in the form of self-knowledge) and the divine Spirit seems to indicate that the receiving of the gift presupposes this capacity. The man who is incapable of receiving and discerning the things of the Spirit of God, and whom Paul describes as the "natural" man (*psychikos*), is not to be thought of as one who is constitutionally devoid of this capacity but rather as one who by his misuse of the freedom of the spirit has forfeited it; for the alternative to receiving the Spirit of God is not complete unspirituality, but to receive the spirit of the world. For Paul it is with our spirit that the Spirit of God bears witness.

3. The theological question, which remains to be considered, is whether we can concede to the human spirit that significance which both philosophical and exegetical considerations seem to demand without coming into collision with the great Protestant and evangelical principle of the sovereignty of grace. The question is thrust upon us in a challenging way by Karl Barth, who has reaffirmed the distinctive emphasis of the Reformers and drawn the consequences with ruthless logic. As we saw in an earlier connection, Barth interprets the *filioque* as precluding not only the notion of a Spirit which proceeds from the Father alone, and which would furnish the basis of a relation between God and man apart from Christ, but also the conception of a created spirit in man. The relation of man to God is established solely and exclusively by the downreach of the Spirit who proceeds from the Father and the Son, i.e., the Spirit who "makes us partakers of the

redemption purchased by Christ." There is no other relation between God and man apart from this, and in this
relation there is no place for the upward reach of a spirit
of man. The question we have to ask is whether *sola gratia*
necessarily entails these two negative consequences.

It may readily be granted that there is no relation between man and God, in the sense of true knowledge of
God and fellowship with God, except in man's personal
encounter with God in Christ. There is no other way in
which we can apprehend God except as he gives himself
to us through Christ in the Holy Spirit. But does it follow
that, apart from this spiritual relation, God and man stand
completely unrelated to each other? Barth holds that the
sovereign sufficiency of the divine act of grace is impugned, should a relation between them be posited in the
order of being. His polemic against the *analogia entis* is
based on the charge that in it " the personal act in which
God turns to man disappears in a relation which subsists
between them all the time." [30] The sovereignty of grace
may seem to be firmly assured in this way, but surely at an
excessive cost. (*a*) If no relation subsists between God and
man all the time, if no ontological or structural relation to
the Creator is implicit in man's creatureliness as such, the
concept of " creature " would seem to be evacuated of all
real meaning. And (*b*), if there is no relation between the
Creator and the creation subsisting all the time, but only
the relation established by the act of grace, it becomes
difficult to maintain the existence of the creation as a
reality *over against* God. In his treatment of the doctrine
of creation, Barth resolves the Berkeleian doubt as to the
existence of the world by merging it in its salvation: *esse
est salvari.*[31] The sovereignty of grace has become totali-
tarianism.

Now with regard to the question of the spirit of man,

Barth does not deny that man has spirit, but, as we have already seen, he equates the spirit of man with the fact that the Spirit of God reaches out toward him. Man is essentially the recipient of spirit, but in no sense the bearer or possessor. The motive again is clear; Barth is concerned, as the Reformers were, to eliminate anything that would suggest that man is capable of making any contribution whatsoever from his side to the divine act of saving grace. Thus the spiritual movement by which the relation between God and man is effected is a movement in one direction exclusively; it consists in the downward reach of the Spirit of God, and there is no place whatsoever for an upward reach of the spirit of man.[32] Barth will allow no kind of *rapprochement* between revelation and religion conceived as a movement of the human spirit, not even when religion is interpreted "as the hand which is stretched out to God and which is then filled by him in his revelation."[33] He will have no "correlation-theology" in any form,[34] and he carries his opposition to the point of refusing even to allow a "proper anthropology"[35]; anthropology is merged in Christology, for man is so utterly dependent on divine grace, not only for his salvation but for his being, that no theological view of him is possible outside this context.[36]

The question that immediately suggests itself here is this: How can human freedom survive in such a situation? Barth's doctrine issues in a kind of universalism which it is hard to reconcile with the reality of human freedom. The decisions of human freedom are in the last analysis overruled by the sovereign decision of divine grace. This has always been the difficulty where *sola gratia* has been affirmed in the sense of the Reformers; Luther's doctrine of the unfreedom of the will and Calvin's doctrine of the double decree were conclusions irresistibly demanded by the logic of grace, as they understood it. And anyone who accepts their premises must needs accept their conclusions.

But does *sola gratia* necessarily entail this consequence? I suggest that, if there be a fallacy here, it should be sought, not in the logic that links the conclusion with the premise (for that is irrefragable), but in the conception of grace that forms the premise of the argument. It was, of course, from Augustine primarily that the Reformers derived their understanding of grace, and its undoubted superiority to that of medieval Catholicism led them to assume that the Augustinian concept of grace is identical with that of the New Testament. Critical scrutiny of the Augustinian concept of grace in the light of the New Testament will show that this is far from being the case.

What is grace? In the New Testament it is used as a comprehensive designation for the act of God in Christ.[37] Grace is that which " came by Jesus Christ " (John 1:17); alternatively, what is extended to men in the gospel can be summarily expressed as "the grace of our Lord Jesus Christ " (II Cor. 8:9). In a word, grace is the meaning of the incarnation. Now Augustine was aware of this; when he wrote about grace he was thinking of the act of God in Christ. But there is one essential element or feature of the incarnation that Augustine failed to incorporate in his concept of grace; for the incarnation involves two elements, both of which must find expression in an adequate concept of grace.

The first is the element of condescension. Augustine saw this clearly, and it was uppermost in the minds of the Reformers, as it is in that of Karl Barth.[38] Grace means primarily that God, whom no man has seen at any time (John 1:18), because he dwells in " the high and holy place " (Isa. 57:15), in the light which no man can approach unto

(I Tim. 6:16), has condescended, has stooped, has come down to man, and has established a relation between himself and man. This aspect of grace may be represented as a vertical line, because it expresses the fact that it is the grace of God, who thus comes down to accomplish his sovereign will on man and who thereby renders all human efforts to "climb the heavenly steeps" and ascend to God redundant and futile. The condescension of the grace of God is clearly indispensable to the realization of his purpose with man. Augustine, however, made the mistake of equating indispensable with irresistible, and he did this because he failed to take account of the other element which is present in the grace of the incarnation, viz., the element of accommodation. For the heart of the gospel is not only that "the only-begotten Son of God . . . of one substance with the Father . . . for us men and for our salvation, came down from heaven," but also that he "was made man"; [39] "Christ Jesus . . . though he was in the form of God," not only "emptied himself," but was also "found in human form" (Phil. 2:5-8); the eternal Word, who "was in the beginning with God," was not only "coming into the world," but also "became flesh and dwelt among us" (John 1:1-14). Augustine saw very clearly that grace is the grace of God who condescends to our level; what he did not see is that precisely as such it is the grace of the Lord Jesus Christ, in whom God confronts us as man, not just descending upon us from above, but coming to meet us at our own level, accommodating himself to our condition.[40] This aspect of grace, which might be represented by a horizontal line, is the opposite of irresistible. It would be nearer the truth to say that its keynote is nonresistance. The incarnate Lord comes as the Son of man, whose mission and destiny it is to be delivered into the hands of man. The grace of the Lord Jesus Christ does

not override man's freedom; it respects it, it engages it to
the full extent, it bows before it, because that is the only
way in which a real relation, i.e., a personal relation between God and man can be realized. Unless man's freedom is engaged, the only relation that could be established between them would be of the I-it order. According
to the Augustinian conception of grace, in which God
descends upon man like an irresistible force, man's role
is only that of an object; significantly enough, it invites
comparison with that of a stock or a stone. But this is a
travesty of the incarnation, which means precisely that
God does not treat man in this impersonal way but ac-
commodates himself to man by taking his form so as to
engage him as a free subject and bring him into a personal
relation with himself. For a personal relationship can be
effected only when man is approached as " thou," i.e., a
subject whose freedom is respected. The incarnation
means not only that God condescends to man, but that
he respects him as man to such an extent that he accepts
the definition of man and subsumes himself under it. If
anthropology were based in Christology, as Barth would
have it, the end term of the incarnation (" and was made
man ") would lack definition. It is the paradox of grace
that God, in descending to man, does not un-man him, as
we might expect, seeing that He is God; by choosing to
become man, He affirms his manhood, He subjects Christology to anthropology.

Now it is fairly evident that the denial of a created spirit
in man, both in ancient and in modern theology, is bound
up with a one-sided, Augustinian conception of grace.
However spirit be conceived, whether it be as a participation in God (as it was in antiquity), or whether it be as
a capacity for God, an affinity with God, an orientation
toward God (as it is currently interpreted in Roman

Catholic theology),[41] or whether it be reduced to a mere "point of contact" for God (as it is by some Protestant theologians), even such a minimal conception seems to be incompatible with the Reformation emphasis on the sufficiency of grace alone. It is on this emphasis that the evangelical power of the gospel depends. But when we speak of the sufficiency of grace alone, we must be careful not to equate it with the sufficiency of that one aspect of grace, which is represented by the vertical line, and lose sight of that other aspect which is represented by the horizontal line. This is the mistake which has too often been made in evangelical theology; evangelical assurance of the sufficiency of grace has been built on what is, in effect, the Catholic conception of grace — differing only from the Catholic conception in that the descending line of grace does not stop at the upward limit of human attainment, but descends to the point at which man lies prostrate before it. But an assurance of grace which involves the virtual suppression of man is not really evangelical. A truly evangelical assurance can be based only on a truly evangelical conception of grace, and that means the grace of the Lord Jesus Christ, the grace of the Word incarnate, the grace which not only descends upon man vertically from above, reducing him to the condition of a helpless target, but which comes to meet him at his own level and engages him at the point of his freedom, which is his spirit.[42]

There is no reason why the existence of a created spirit in man, as distinct from the immanence of the Spirit of God in him, should be thought to conflict with the sufficiency of grace alone, if the nature of spirit and its activity be properly understood. It is the conception of spirit as the principle of a relation to God immanent in man, or as itself divine, which makes such a conflict inevitable. Plainly this conception cannot be entertained in Christian thought; there can be no immanent principle of a relation to God in sinful man. But, while sin alienates man from God, this does not mean that there is no spirit in man. Man remains a being endowed with created spirit (for spirit is the distinctive mark of man, and without it he would not be man); but spirit in sinful man becomes the principle of his *lost* relation to God; for man's relation to God is always a relation in freedom, and spirit is the principle of freedom.

In the order of creation man is a being destined for fellowship with God, and, since this is a relation to be realized in freedom, man, as God's creature, is endowed with freedom in the form of created spirit. The image of God in man becomes intelligible when it is understood in this sense, not as indicating some kind of affinity with God inherent in man's creaturely structure, but as a relation freely willed by God and to be received by man in freedom.[43] Now, when this relation is realized in the free correspondence of created with uncreated Spirit, the communion between them is of such a nature that, while the human spirit is not displaced by the divine, it is so open and receptive to the divine that it gladly yields place to it. In the experience which is described in the New Testament as the communion of the Holy Spirit, man's spirit does not lose its distinctness; for " the Spirit itself beareth witness with our spirit, that we are the children of God " (Rom. 8:16); yet its own distinctness is that of which the human spirit is least conscious, and the man who is in communion with the Holy Spirit is described as " filled with the Holy Spirit " (Acts 9:17; Eph. 5:18). This sheds some light on the preference of theology for dichotomy over trichotomy; the realized relation between God and man is more naturally expressed in dichotomous language.[44] But dichotomous language is hardly adequate to describe the condition of sinful man, who is not in communion with God. Irenaeus was one who identified the spirit of man with the presence of the Spirit of God in him, and he associated it particularly with the "likeness" (or "similitude"), which he distinguished from the "image" of God; since the Fall, in his view, involved the loss of the likeness (but not the image), fallen man became a being without spirit at all, a being of animal or carnal nature.[45] The fall is conceived as a fall into dichotomy. But is fallen man really a being without spirit? Is it not precisely in fallen man, the man whose communion with God is broken, that the human spirit comes to consciousness of itself in its distinctness from the Spirit of God? It would seem to be more plausible to represent the Fall as a fall into trichotomy, not in the sense that spirit becomes distinct from soul at the Fall, but that they no longer point in the same direction.[46] The structure of man's being, i.e., the dependence of his creaturely existence (his soul) upon God, remains unchanged; but his *relation* to God is changed, inasmuch as his created spirit no longer responds in freedom to the Spirit of God. Yet spirit remains spirit, and the essential quality and dimension of spiritual activity continue to manifest themselves in sinful man.

As the faculty of self-transcendence, as freedom to relate himself to that which is beyond himself, the presence of spirit in man manifests itself to a phenomenological view. Inasmuch as spirit in sinful man has lost its creational "orientation toward God" and has become a "capacity for indeterminate self-transcendence," [47] sinful man may be said to have lost the image of God. But inasmuch as spirit continues to be present in sinful man and, indeed, to constitute the most distinctive feature about him, the being of man retains its essentially *image*-character; and the activity of spirit, which is free, may be interpreted both philosophically, as the quest for universal truth and value,[48] the aspiration after that which is meaningful and normative,[49] and theologically, as the search for the God man has lost through his sin. Berdyaev expressed the plight of man in the phrase, "Man has lost his image," but it would be more appropriate to say that he has lost his original, of which he is the image; for the presence of spirit in man is the index of the essentially image-character of his being.

In this way it seems possible for Christian theology to recognize the element of truth in the Platonic doctrine of *anamnesis* and the description of the spirit's activity as *eros;* for *eros,* as the child of *poros* (plenty) and *penia* (poverty), represents the longing for a lost fullness. This significance can be accorded to the human spirit without fear of compromising the essential evangelical doctrine of *sola gratia;* for it does not mean an inherent capacity for God which is unimpaired by sin; it is in the freedom of his spirit that man changes his freedom *for* God to a freedom *from* God. But man cannot in the freedom of his spirit reverse this change. That is the essential limitation upon the freedom of his spirit as created. Created spirit cannot choose the Creator as a possibility. The restoration of man's relation to God involves the abnegation of all the possibilities of created spirit, the acknowledgment of his poverty of spirit, the sacrifice of a broken and a contrite spirit, and the gift of the Holy Spirit. The Holy Spirit does not annihilate our spirits, but bears witness with our spirits. And the Holy Spirit does not destroy the freedom of our spirits, but restores it by changing their false freedom from God into that true freedom for God, which is "the glorious liberty of the children of God."

Notes

Chapter 1

[1] A. R. Vidler, *Christian Belief,* pp. 55 f. Charles Scribner's Sons, 1950.

[2] One of the most widely read treatments of the Spirit in recent years, *The Christian Experience of the Holy Spirit* (James Nisbet & Co., Ltd., London, 1928), was, significantly the work of an Old Testament scholar, H. Wheeler Robinson.

[3] Cf. A. E. J. Rawlinson, *The New Testament Doctrine of the Christ,* p. 115. Longmans, London, 1926.

[4] Büchsel, *Der Geist Gottes im Neuen Testament,* p. 409. Gütersloh, Bertelsmann, 1926.

[5] Cf. H. B. Swete, *The Holy Spirit in the New Testament,* p. 388. The Macmillan Company, London, 1909.

[6] Cf. C. H. Dodd, *According to the Scriptures.* Charles Scribner's Sons, 1953.

Chapter 2

[1] Cf. Hoskyns' Commentary (Faber and Faber, London, 1947) on this passage and on John 1:51, and Eduard Schweizer, *Geist und Gemeinde im Neuen Testament und heute* (*Theologische Existenz heute,* N. F. 32), pp. 27 f. Kaiser, München, 1952.

[2] Feine, *Theologie des Neuen Testaments,* p. 261. Seventh edition, Hinrichs, Leipzig, 1936.

[3] The historical mystery surrounding the origin of the "Niceno-Constantinopolitan Creed" does not concern us here. For an admirable discussion of it, see J. N. D. Kelly, *Early Christian Creeds,* pp. 296 ff. Longmans, London, 1950.

[4] Translation from Kelly, *op. cit.,* p. 298.

[5] Cf. Kelly, *op. cit.,* pp. 342 f.

[6] Kelly, *op. cit.,* p. 296.

[7] For the history of the Western interpolation, see Kelly, *op. cit.,* pp. 358–367.

[8] I have attempted to appraise it in an article, "From the Father and the Son: The *Filioque* After Nine Hundred Years," in *Theology Today,* XI, 4, pp. 449–459.

[9] Martin Kähler, " Das schriftmässige Bekenntnis zum Geiste Christi," in *Dogmatische Zeitfragen,* I, pp. 137–176. Deichertsche Verlagsbuchhandlung, Leipzig, 1908.

[10] Karl Barth, *Kirchliche Dogmatik,* I, 1, pp. 500–511; Claude Welch, " The Holy Spirit and the Trinity," in *Theology Today,* VIII, 1 (1951), pp. 29–40; Carl Michalson, " The Holy Spirit and the Church," *ibid.,* pp. 41–54; Claude Welch, *In This Name,* Index, *s.v. Filioque.* Charles Scribner's Sons, 1952.

[11] Barth, *op. cit.,* p. 503.

[12] Welch, *In This Name,* p. 184.

[13] *Op. cit.,* p. 285.

[14] There is a full discussion of it in Welch's book.

[15] Augustine, *De Trinitate,* 5, 12. Origen's comment on John 4:24, " God is spirit," is: " Here it is said that *pneuma* is, as is were, his *ousia* (*Comm. in Jo.,* XIII, 21–23, ed., Brooke, I, pp. 267–270).

[16] *Theology Today,* VIII, 1, p. 29.

[17] The naïve way is by a simple " both . . . and." Cf. Calvin, *Inst.,* III, 1, 2.

[18] *The Christian Understanding of God,* p. 44. Harper & Brothers, 1951.

[19] *Op. cit.,* p. 197.

[20] All quotations are from Tillich, *Systematic Theology,* I, pp. 250 f. University of Chicago Press, 1951. Compare the very similar position taken by Boulgakof: " God is Spirit in his tri-personal being. . . . At the same time the spirituality in God is expressly attributed to the Holy Spirit, because it is the Holy Spirit who manifests the spirituality of the Trinity. . . . Similarly the Holy Spirit realizes the spirituality which belongs to each of the hypostases. . . . In this way the Holy Spirit is both a single and a triple hypostasis " (*Le Paraclet,* pp. 145 ff. Aubier, Paris, 1946).

[21] Barth, *Kirchliche Dogmatik,* III, 1, pp. 51–59.

[22] *Op. cit.,* p. 44 (*Leitsatz*).

[23] *Op. cit.,* pp. 59–63.

[24] *Op. cit.,* III, 2, p. 431.

[25] *Op. cit.,* I, 2, p. 269.

[26] *Op. cit.,* III, 2, pp. 428 ff.

[27] *Loc. cit.,* p. 458.

Chapter 3

[1] A. R. Vidler, *Christian Belief*, p. 73. Charles Scribner's Sons, 1950.
[2] The Church: Report of a Theological Commission on Faith and Order, 1951, p. 58. S.C.M. Press, London, 1951.
[3] Faith and Order: The Report of the Third World Conference at Lund, Sweden, August 15–28, 1952, p. 11. S.C.M. Press, 1952.
[4] *The Gospel and the Catholic Church*. Longmans, London, 1936.
[5] *Divinum illud*, June 20, 1896.
[6] *Mystici corporis*, June 29, 1943.
[7] Cf. Congar, *Divided Christendom*, p. 57 (Geoffrey Bles, Ltd., London, 1939), and *Mystici corporis* (edition of National Catholic Welfare Conference), pp. 21 f.
[8] *Satis cognitum*, June 20, 1896, cited from *The Great Encyclicals of Leo XIII*, pp. 351 ff. Benziger Brothers, New York, 1903.
[9] Cf. *Divinum illud, op. cit., supra*, p. 422.
[10] *Mystici corporis*, p. 9.
[11] *Ibid.*, p. 15.
[12] Leo XIII, *op. cit.*, p. 355.
[13] *Mystici corporis*, p. 30.
[14] Congar, *op. cit.*, p. 26.
[15] *Mystici corporis*, p. 9.
[16] *Ibid.*, p. 22.
[17] A. M. Ramsey, *The Gospel and the Catholic Church*, p. 69. Longmans, London, 1936.
[18] *Op. cit.*, p. 77.
[19] *The Apostolic Ministry*. Hodder & Stoughton, Ltd., London, 1946.
[20] *Op. cit.*, pp. 82 f.
[21] Cf. Newbigin, *The Reunion of the Church*, pp. 163 f. S.C.M. Press, London, 1948.
[22] *Op. cit.*, p. 183.
[23] *Op. cit.*, p. 61. Cf. the similar judgment of Hermann Diem: "The Church takes the gospel under its own management, so that there can be no confrontation between it and the Word of God, and its preaching becomes a mere conversa-

tion with itself." *Theologie als kirchliche Wissenschaft,* p. 19. Kaiser, München, 1951.

24 Cf. Barth, *Kirchliche Dogmatik,* IV, 1, p. 803.

25 *Op. cit.,* pp. 351 f. Cf. pp. 361 f., where we have an even cruder statement of the papal conception of the "institution of Christianity": "Christ proves his own divinity and the divine origin of his mission by miracles; he teaches the multitudes heavenly doctrine by word of mouth; and he absolutely commands that the assent of faith should be given to his teaching, promising eternal rewards to those who believe and eternal punishment to those who do not [the pope cites John 10:37; 15:24; 10:38]. . . . When about to ascend into heaven he sends his apostles in virtue of the same power by which he had been sent from the Father; and he charges them to spread abroad and propagate his teaching [Matt. 28:18–20]. . . . But since it is obviously most in harmony with God's providence that no one should have confided to him a great and important mission unless he were furnished with the means of properly carrying it out, for this reason Christ promised that he would send the Spirit of truth to his disciples to remain with them forever."

26 *Op. cit.,* p. 91. Cf. p. 69: "Thus the Church on earth follows this law of incarnation."

27 Cf. Augsburg Confession, Art. V: "In order that we may obtain this faith [by which we are justified] there has been instituted the ministry of preaching the gospel and dispensing the sacraments. For it is through the Word and sacraments as means that the Holy Spirit is given, who produces faith, as and when it seems good to God, in those who hear the gospel."

28 *Mystici corporis,* p. 21.

29 *Inst.,* III, 2, 6.

30 This phrase, which was first used of the Eucharist, is more commonly applied to the Church in the Anglican communion. Efforts to trace its origin have so far proved unsuccessful. (See correspondence in the Anglican journal, *Theology,* July, 1952.)

31 Congar, *op. cit.,* p. 69. Congar cites the law of incarnation as the ground of the divine-human character of the Church. He does not expressly relate it to the principle of historical

continuity; but this is a commonplace in Roman theology.

[32] Not vertically from above, as we should perhaps expect, but from below. The Spirit arises out of the depths of the soul. This was the teaching of Münzer and Denck.

Chapter 4

[1] *Conf. Aug.*, Art. V, *De Ministerio Ecclesiastico.*
Ut hanc fidem consequamur, institutum est ministerium docendi evangelii et porrigendi sacramenta. Nam per verbum, et sacramenta tamquam per instrumenta donatur Spiritus Sanctus, qui fidem efficit, ubi et quando visum est Deo, in iis qui audiunt evangelium.

[2] *Cat. Genev.*, pp. 301–307 (*Bekenntnisschriften der reformierten Kirche*, ed. Niesel, p. 34). Kaiser, München, 1938.

[3] *Op. cit.*, p. 223.

[4] A. 89.

[5] *Inst.*, I, 9, 3.

[6] *Inst.*, I, 7, 4 f.

[7] *Inst.*, I, 7, 2.

[8] Westminster Confession, I, 5.

[9] *Ego vero evangelio non crederem, nisi me catholicae ecclesiae commoveret auctoritas. Contra ep., Manich.*, 5, 6.

[10] *Inst.*, I, 7, 3. Had Augustine meant what Calvin says, he would surely have expressed himself differently: " I should not *have believed* . . . unless I *had been influenced* . . ."; i.e., he would have written: *Credidissem . . . commovisset.* I owe this point to Loofs, *Dogmengeschichte* (4th ed.), p. 369. Niemeyer, Halle, 1906.
It is interesting to compare the role which Calvin, somewhat grudgingly, allows to the Church in this context with that which he assigns to it in his extended treatment of the doctrine of the Church in *Inst.*, IV, 1, 1. There the Church appears as the mother " in whose bosom it is God's will that his sons should be gathered, not only to be nourished by her labor and ministry while they are infants and children, but to be governed by her maternal care until they grow up and at length attain to the goal of their faith." Here the Church seems rather to play the part of the father of the bride who hands her over to the bridegroom and then retires discreetly into the background.

[12] *Inst.*, I, 7, 5.
[13] In his comment on John 11:49, Calvin rejects the view that the prophecy of Caiaphas is to be ascribed to "mechanical" inspiration: "He did not utter an unintelligible sound like a person in a trance or ecstasy (*tamquam arrepticus et fanaticus*); he spoke according to his own understanding: but the Evangelist means that his tongue was under a higher direction, because God willed that something higher than what was in his own mind should be attested by his mouth. Caiaphas was, so to speak, bilingual at that moment."
[14] *Obsolescence of Oracles*, 432. Reprinted by permission of the publishers from Loeb Classical Library.
[15] *Phaedrus*, 244A. Plato thought *mantike* (prophecy) was derived from *mania* (madness). Reprinted by permission of the publishers from Loeb Classical Library.
[16] *Ion*, 533 Df. Reprinted by permission of the publishers from Loeb Classical Library.
[17] Philo, *Who Is the Heir?* 259. Cf. *Special Laws*, IV, 49: "For no pronouncement of a prophet is ever his own; he is an interpreter prompted by another in all his utterances, when not knowing what he does he is filled with inspiration, as the reason withdraws and surrenders the citadel of the soul to a new visitor and tenant, the divine Spirit which plays upon the vocal organism and dictates words which clearly express its prophetic message." While Plato extended such inspiration to the poets, Philo believed it to be of frequent occurrence in his own experience as a writer of prose — many writers will recognize a familiar experience in the description he gives: "For the offspring of the soul's own travail are for the most part poor abortions, things untimely born, but those which God waters with the snows of heaven come to the birth perfect, complete and peerless. I feel no shame in recording my own experience, a thing I know from its having happened to me a thousand times. On some occasions, after having made up my mind to follow the usual course of writing on philosophical tenets, and knowing definitely the substance of what I was to set down, I have found my understanding incapable of giving birth to a single idea, and have given it up without accomplishing anything, reviling my understanding for its self-conceit, and

filled with amazement at the might of Him who is, and to
whom is due the opening and closing of the soul wombs.
On other occasions I have approached my work empty and
suddenly become full, the ideas falling in a shower from
above and being sown invisibly, so that under the influence
of the divine possession I have been filled with corybantic
frenzy and been unconscious of anything, place, persons present, myself, words spoken, lines written. For I obtained
language, ideas, and enjoyment of light, keenest vision,
pellucid distinctness of objects, such as might be received
through the eyes as the result of clearest showing" (*Migra-
tion of Abraham,* 33 ff.). Reprinted by permission of the
publishers from Loeb Classical Library.

[18] Cf. Volz, *Der Geist Gottes,* p. 168. Mohr, Tübingen, 1910.
The change was accompanied by an intellectualization of
the content of revelation and the elevation of the "intellectual" (in the form of the scribe) as its interpreter. The
trend is already apparent in the wisdom literature of the
Old Testament, where the great alternative of the blessing
and the curse, of good and evil, of life and death, is presented in terms of wisdom and folly, and the path of life is
paved with knowledge and instruction and understanding
and learning. It is more pronounced in the apocryphal literature belonging to the same type. Ecclesiasticus surveys the
various employments of mankind and assesses their relative
importance in the scheme of things: the physician is to be
honored, because healing, in which he is skilled, comes from
the Most High; the farmer, whose mind is all on his fields
and his beasts, "and whose discourse is of the stock of
bulls," the smith sweating in front of his forge with the
noise of the hammer continually in his ears, the potter
pedaling away at his wheel — all these "maintain the fabric
of the world." But their place is inferior. The highest place
belongs to the scribe, who "by opportunity of leisure" has
applied himself to the study of the Law and the Prophets
and the wisdom of the ancients and has become an acknowledged authority in the interpretation of them; he will make
himself an immortal name by his understanding — for such
is the Spirit with which he shall be filled (Ecclus., chs.
38; 39).

[19] Philo, *Life of Moses*, II, 37.

[20] Cf. Calvin, *Inst.*, I, 7, 2.

[21] Cf. Theo Preiss, *Das innere Zeugnis des heiligen Geistes*, p. 11. Evangelische Verlag, Zürich, 1947.

[22] Art. 4: *Nous cognoissons ces livres estre Canoniques, et la reigle trescertaine de nostre foy* (Pseau. 19, 8 et 9): *non tant par le commun accord et consentement de l'Eglise, que par le tesmoignage et persuasion interieure du sainct Esprit, qui les nous fait discerner d'avec les authres livres Ecclesiastiques, sur lesquels, encore qu'ils soyent utiles, on ne peut fonder aucun article de foy* (Niesel, *op. cit.*, p. 67).

[23] Cf. Westminster Confession, I, 3.

[24] Cited in H. Cunliffe-Jones, *The Authority of the Biblical Revelation*, p. 68. James Clarke, Ltd., London, 1945.

[25] Quenstedt, a classic exponent of Lutheran orthodoxy, tries to emphasize the difference between the inspiration of the Bible and such pagan conceptions — but it amounts to no more than the difference between a stenographer and a typewriter (Schmid, *Dogmatik der ev.-luth. Kirche*, p. 21. Bertelsmann, Gütersloh, 1893).

[26] Cf. Theo Preiss, *op. cit.*, p. 26.

[27] *Confessions of an Inquiring Spirit*, Letter I. Bell, London, 1913.

[28] Milligan, *The New Testament Documents*, pp. 227 f. (quoted in H. Wheeler Robinson, *The Christian Experience of the Holy Spirit*, p. 179).

[29] Cf. H. Cunliffe-Jones, *op. cit.*, p. 94.

[30] The romantic nature of the appeal of Scripture to Coleridge is evident from his description of what he found in it — "copious sources of truth, and power and purifying impulses" (*loc. cit.*). The appeal can also be of a literary and aesthetic order; indeed, the number of people for whom the appeal of the Bible is bound up with the stately Elizabethan English of the Authorized Version is probably greater than we should imagine.

[31] Kierkegaard, *Philosophical Fragments*, p. 87. Princeton University Press, 1936.

Chapter 5

[1] Cf. Eisler, *Wörterbuch der philosophischen Begriffe*, I, p. 485 (E. S. Mittler, Berlin, 1927–1930), and Wili, "Die Ge-

schichte des Geistes in der Antike," *Eranos Jahrbuch,* 1945, p. 58. Rhein-Verlag, Zürich, 1945.

² *Conf.,* I, 1.

³ *De civ. dei,* VIII, 4.

⁴ *Cont. gent.,* III, 25, etc.

⁵ For a good example in contemporary Roman Catholic theology, see Michael Schmaus, *Katholische Dogmatik,* II, pp. 277 ff. Hochschulverlag Hueber, München, 1949.

⁶ WA, 7, p. 550.

⁷ *Symbolische Bücher der ev.-luth. Kirche,* ed., J. T. Müller, p. 358. Bertelsmann, Gütersloh, 1898.

⁸ WA, 7, p. 551.

⁹ *Symbolische Bücher der ev.-luth. Kirche,* p. 593.

¹⁰ *Inst.,* I, 15, 6.

¹¹ Cf. *Comm.* on John 14:1.

¹² *Inst.,* II, 4, 1.

¹³ Cf. *West. Conf.,* X, 2 and IX, 3.

¹⁴ *West. Conf.,* X, 2.

¹⁵ VI, p. 599, quoted by H. Barth in " Die Geistfrage im deutschen Idealismus," in *Zur Lehre vom Heiligen Geist,* p. 17. Kaiser, München, 1930.

¹⁶ Scheler, *Die Stellung des Menschen im Kosmos,* p. 48. Nymphenburger Verlagshandlung, München, 1947.

¹⁷ Cf. George F. Thomas, *Spirit and Its Freedom.* University of North Carolina Press, 1939.

¹⁸ *Nature and Destiny of Man,* I, pp. 3 f. Charles Scribner's Sons, 1943.

¹⁹ H. H. Farmer, *Towards Belief in God,* pp. 74 f. S.C.M. Press, London, 1942.

²⁰ Niebuhr, *op. cit.,* p. 14. Scheler traces a connection between man's ability to conceive the empty forms of space and time and his experience of emptiness in his intercourse with the world of space and time. " Empty is the name we give originally to the unfulfillment of our impulsive expectations — the first void, so to speak, is the void of our own hearts." *Op. cit.,* p. 46.

²¹ Brunner, *Man in Revolt,* p. 238. The Westminster Press, 1947.

²² *Op. cit.,* p. 49.

²³ Niebuhr, *op. cit.,* I, p. 162.

[24] Eichrodt, *Theologie des Alten Testaments*, 2, p. 19, n. 10. Hinrichs, Leipzig, 1935.

[25] Bultmann, *Theologie des Neuen Testaments*, p. 203. Mohr, Tübingen, 1948.

[26] *Op. cit.*, p. 20.

[27] Cf. Barth, *KD*, III, 1, pp. 267 ff. For Schmaus, the human spirit is the focal point of the image of God: "It is in his spirit that man is the image of God, that he bears the lineaments of God, that he is akin to God" (*Katholische Dogmatik*, 2, p. 332).

[28] Bultmann, *op. cit.*, pp. 205 f.

[29] Cf. Scheler, *op. cit.*, p. 87.

[30] *KD*, I, 1, p. 40.

[31] *KD*, III, 1, pp. 1 ff.

[32] *KD*, III, 2, pp. 414–440.

[33] *KD*, I, 2, p. 330.

[34] *KD*, I, 1, p. 179.

[35] *KD*, I, 1, pp. 130 ff.

[36] *KD*, III, 2, p. 43.

[37] But it is not the only one; and the similar use of other terms, such as truth (John 1:17), faith (Gal. 3:25), love (Rom. 8:39), life (I John 1:2), serves as a warning against pressing any one term too far.

[38] *KD*, II, 1, p. 398.

[39] Nicene Creed.

[40] For Augustine, grace is the grace of God the Father Almighty, rather than the grace of the Lord Jesus Christ. Cf. Harnack, *DG*, III, p. 217 (Mohr, Tübingen, 1910): "*Dass die Gnade gratia per Christum sei, hat Augustin keineswegs so sicher festgehalten, wie dass sie aus dem verborgenen Wirken Gottes stamme.*"

[41] Cf. Schmaus, *Katholische Dogmatik*, 2, pp. 277 ff.

[42] The necessity for a revision of the conception of grace in Protestant theology was first urged by John Oman in *Grace and Personality* (Cambridge University Press, London, 1917). In this book, which was first published in 1917, the distinction between the I-thou and the I-it relationship, which was to receive its classical exposition at the hands of Martin Buber six years later, was already drawn and applied to theological thinking.

[43] Niebuhr points out the importance of making a distinction between the essential nature of man and the virtue of conformity to it: "Man may lose this virtue and destroy the proper function of his nature, but he can do so only by availing himself of one of the elements in that nature, namely this freedom" (*Nature and Destiny of Man*, I, p. 286). For an example of the difficulties presented by this distinction in theological thinking in which the existence of created spirit, and its freedom, is not recognized, see Barth, *Zur Lehre vom Heiligen Geist*, p. 45, n. 19. This would be the decisive reason for rejecting Barth's identification of the image of God in man with the relation between man and woman (*KD*, III, 1, pp. 204–231); for the latter is inherent in his physiological structure and is, as such, a relation of necessity, to say nothing of the fact that it is common to man and other members of the animal creation. Yet, inasmuch as the relation between man and woman reaches the distinctively human level only when a free or spiritual relation is superimposed on the structural relation, it may be taken as an analogy or image of the image of God in man.

[44] In his discussion of dichotomy and trichotomy, Delitzsch says that the "dichotomic view according to which Scripture knows nothing of a created spirit . . . is an actual proof of the strong impression made by the assumption that governs the *usus loquendi* of Scripture, that the created spirit of man is a spirit that proceeds from God" (*Biblical Psychology*, p. 107. Clark, Edinburgh, 1869).

[45] *Adv. Haer.*, V. 6, 1.

[46] Cf. Delitzsch, *op. cit.*, p. 114: "The essential difference between a human nature-psyche and the human thinking spirit is an invention contrary to Scripture and to experience. The dualism of *psyche* and *pneuma*, under which man, considered ethically, is groaning, is a consequence of sin, which has disunited in itself his life-principle which he had received immediately from God."

[47] The phrases are taken from Niebuhr, *op. cit.*, pp. 163 f.

[48] Thomas, *op. cit.*, p. 49.

[49] Brunner, *op. cit.*, p. 238.